1
First Grade
Essentials

Thinking Kids®
Carson-Dellosa Publishing LLC
Greensboro, North Carolina

Thinking Kids®
An imprint of Carson-Dellosa Publishing LLC
P.O. Box 35665
Greensboro, NC 27425 USA

Printed in the USA • All rights reserved.   ISBN 978-1-4838-3818-2

01-135171151

Table of Contents

INTRODUCTION

Welcome to the *Essentials* series!

Building a strong foundation is an essential part of your child's everyday success. This series features a variety of activity pages that make learning fun, keeping your child engaged and entertained at the same time. These colorful workbooks will help children meet important proficiency standards with activities that strengthen their basic skills, math, and reading.

With the *Essentials* series, learning isn't just contained to the pages of the workbook. Each activity offers "One Step Further," a suggestion for children to continue the learning activity on their own. This encourages children to take what they've learned and apply it to everyday situations, reinforcing their comprehension of the activity while exploring the world around them, preparing them with the skills needed to succeed in the 21st century.

These books provide an outstanding educational experience and important learning tools to prepare your child for the future. The *Essentials* series offers hours of educational entertainment that will make your child want to come back for more!

Basic Skills

TALL

TALLEST

TALLER

ABC Order

Directions: Circle the first letter of each word. Then, put each pair of the words in **ABC** order.

ⓒar   ⓑird   moon   two   nest   fan

bird

car

card   dog   pig   bike   sun   pie

One Step Further

Write three words. Ask a friend to put them in ABC order.

ABC Order

ABC Order

Directions: Look at the words in each box. Circle the word that comes first in **ABC** order.

duck
four
rock

chair
apple
yellow

peach
this
walk

game
boy
pink

light
come
one

mouse
ten
orange

angel
table
hair

zebra
watch
five

foot
boat
mine

look
blue
rope

who
dog
black

book
tan
six

One Step Further
Write down names of your friends and family.
Can you put them in ABC order?

Rhyming Words

Rhyming words are words that sound alike at the end of the word. **Cat** and **hat** rhyme.

Directions: Draw a circle around each word pair that rhymes. Draw an **X** on each pair that does **not** rhyme.

Example:

(soap rope)	red dog	book hook
cold rock	cat hat	yellow black
one two	rock sock	rat flat
good nice	you to	meet toy
old sold	sale whale	word letter

One Step Further

Choose two rhyming words from this page.
Find objects that show their meanings.

Rhyming Words

Rhyming words are words that sound alike at the end of the word.

Directions: Draw a line to match the pictures that rhyme. Write two of your rhyming word pairs below.

- - - - - - - - - - - - - - - - - - - -

- - - - - - - - - - - - - - - - - - - -

One Step Further
What word rhymes with your name?
Make up a word if you have to!

These Keep Me Warm

Directions: Color the things that keep you warm.

socks

apple

lunch box

earmuffs

cookie

coat

umbrella

hat

gloves

book

One Step Further
What do you do when you are cold?
What clothes do you wear during the winter?

Food Groups

Directions: Color the meats and eggs **brown**. Color the fruits and vegetables **green**. Color the breads **tan**. Color the dairy foods (milk and cheese) yellow.

fish

bread

apple

cheese

crackers

carrot

orange

eggs

steak

pear

milk

yogurt

ice cream

chicken

potato

pretzel

One Step Further

What is your favorite food from each of these food groups?

BASIC SKILLS

Things That Go Together

Directions: Draw a line to connect the things that go together.

toothpaste

washcloth

pencil

sock

salt

toothbrush

shoe

pepper

soap

paper

One Step Further

Look around your home.
Find two more things that go together.

Things That Go Together

Directions: Draw a line to connect the things that go together.

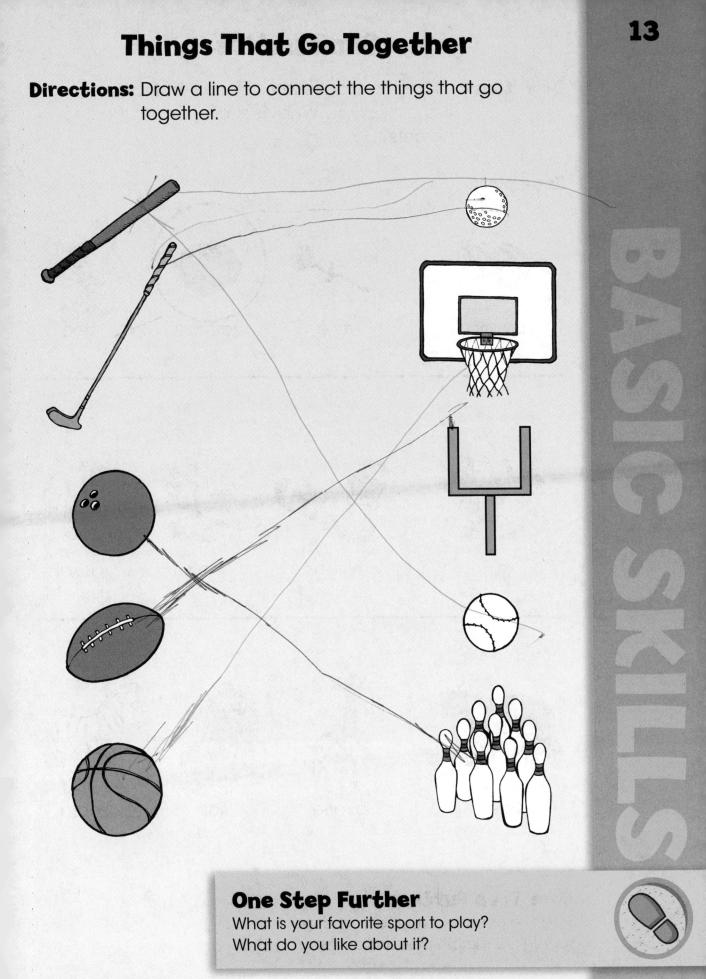

One Step Further
What is your favorite sport to play?
What do you like about it?

Similarities

Directions: Circle the picture in each row that is most like the first picture. What is similar about the two objects?

Example:

potato	rose	tomato	tree

shirt	mittens	boots	jacket

tiger	giraffe	lion	zebra

One Step Further

Find two objects in your room that go together. Describe their similarities.

Similarities

Directions: Circle the picture in each row that is most like the first picture. What is similar about the two objects?

Example:

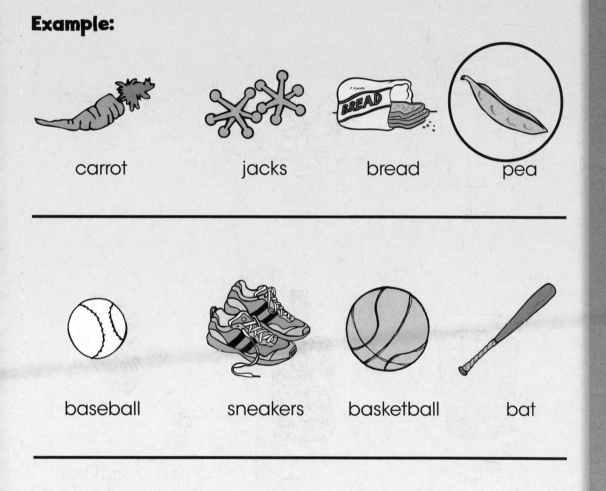

carrot   jacks   bread   pea

baseball   sneakers   basketball   bat

store   school   home   bakery

One Step Further
What is your favorite store?
Name another store that is similar.

First Grade Essentials

Things to Drink

Directions: Circle the pictures of things you can drink. Write the names of those things in the blanks.

milk   ice   soup and crackers

juice   soda   ice-cream bar

One Step Further

Name something else you can drink.
What is your favorite thing to drink?

Clowns and Balloons

Some words describe clowns. Some words describe balloons.

Directions: Read the words. Write the words in the correct columns.

float	hat	air	pop
laughs	string	feet	nose

_____

_____

_____

_____

_____

_____

_____

_____

One Step Further
How else could you describe a clown?
Tell a story about a clown to a friend.

Vocabulary

Directions: Read the words. Trace and write them on the lines. Look at each picture. Write **hot** or **cold** on the lines to show if it is hot or cold.

hot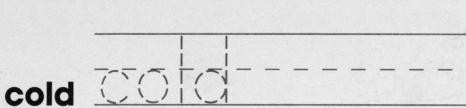

cold

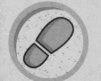

One Step Further
What foods are hot? What foods are cold?
Which of these foods do you like best?

BASIC SKILLS

Vocabulary

Directions: Read the words. Trace and write them on the lines. Look at each picture. Write **day** or **night** on the lines to show if they happen during the day or night.

day

day ----------

night

night --------------

One Step Further

What do you do during the day?
What do you do at night?

What Does Not Belong?

Directions: Draw an **X** on the picture that does **not** belong in each group.

fruit

apple

peach

corn

watermelon

wild animals

bear

kitten

gorilla

lion

flowers

grass

rose

daisy

tulip

One Step Further

Name another object that belongs in each category on this page. Draw the objects.

BASIC SKILLS

What Does Not Belong?

Directions: Draw an **X** on the word in each row that does **not** belong.

1. flashlight   candle   radio   fire

2. shirt   pants   coat   bat

3. cow   car   bus   train

4. beans   hot dog   ball   bread

5. gloves   hat   book   boots

6. fork   butter   cup   plate

One Step Further
Tell a story about a camping trip.
Make up characters for your story.

BASIC SKILLS

Things That Belong Together

Directions: Circle the pictures in each row that belong together.

Row 1   cookies   cake   beans   ice cream

Row 2   kite   dice   checkers   chess

Directions: Write the names of the things that do **not** belong. Why do these pictures not belong?

_____

- - - - - - - - - - - - - - - - - - - -

Row 1 _____

_____

- - - - - - - - - - - - - - - - - - - -

Row 2 _____

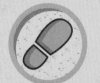

One Step Further

Name a game you can play on a rainy day.
Draw it here.

Where Does It Belong?

Directions: Read the words.
Draw a **circle** around the **sky words**.
Draw a **line** under the **land words**.
Draw a **box** around the **sea words**.

city	rabbit	planet
cloud	forest	whale
shark	moon	shell

Directions: Write each word on the correct line.

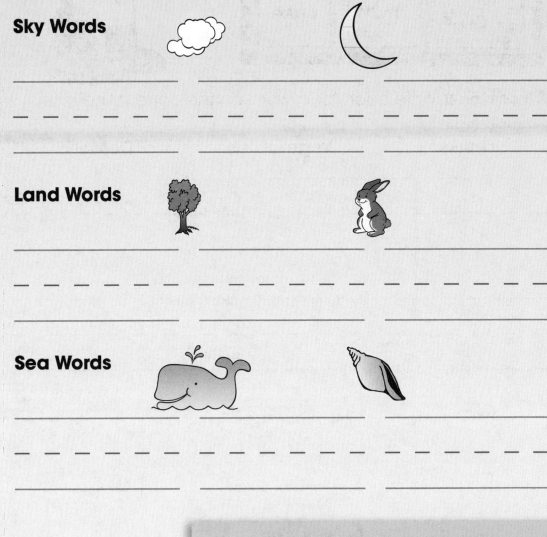

Sky Words

_____ _____ _____

Land Words

_____ _____ _____

Sea Words

_____ _____ _____

One Step Further

Walk around your neighborhood.
What other land words could you add?

BASIC SKILLS

Menu Mix-Up

Directions: Circle names of **drinks** in **red**.
Circle names of **vegetables** in green.
Circle names of **desserts** in pink.

Directions: Write each food word on the correct line.

Drinks	Vegetables	Desserts

One Step Further

Pretend you own a restaurant.
What would be on your menu?

Word Sort

Directions: Circle words that name **colors** in **red**.
Circle words that name **shapes** in yellow.
Circle words that name **numbers** in **green**.

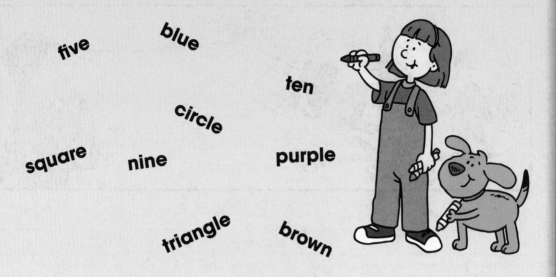

five

blue

ten

circle

square   nine   purple

triangle   brown

Directions: Write each word on the correct line.

Colors	Shapes	Numbers

One Step Further

Sort your clothes based on color.
What color is the biggest group?

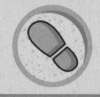

BASIC SKILLS

What Does Not Belong?

Directions: Circle the two things that do not belong in the picture. Write why they do not belong.

1. _____

2. _____

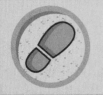

One Step Further
Describe what is happening in the picture.
What winter activities do you enjoy?

Classification

Directions: The words in each box form a group. Choose the word from the word box that describes each group and write it on the line.

clothes	family	colors
flowers	fruits	animals
coins	toys	noises

rose
buttercup
tulip
daisy

_____

crash
bang
ring
pop

_____

mother
father
sister
brother

_____

puzzle
wagon
blocks
doll

_____

green
purple
blue
red

_____

grapes
orange
apple
plum

_____

shirt
socks
dress
coat

_____

dime
penny
nickel
quarter

_____

dog
horse
elephant
moose

_____

One Step Further

Look in your closet or drawer. What other words could be classified as clothes?

First Grade Essentials

Raking Leaves

Directions: Write a number in each box to show the order of the story.

One Step Further

Go outside and find 10 leaves.
What color are the leaves?

Make a Snowman!

Directions: Write the number of the sentence that goes with each picture in the box.

1. Roll a large snowball for the snowman's bottom.
2. Make another snowball and put it on top of the first.
3. Put the last snowball on top.
4. Dress the snowman.

One Step Further

Tell a story about building a snowman.
Have you ever built a snowman?

Color the Path

Directions: Color the path the girl should take to go home.
Use the sentences to help you.

1. Go to the school and turn left.
2. At the end of the street, turn right.
3. Walk past the park and turn right.
4. After you pass the pool, turn right.

One Step Further

Create a map of your neighborhood.
Be sure to label your house and your street!

Directions: Look at the pictures. Follow the directions in each box.

Draw a circle around the caterpillar. Draw a line under the stick.

Draw an **X** on the mother bird. Draw a triangle around the baby birds.

Draw a box around the rabbit.

Color the flowers. Count the bees. There are _____ bees.

One Step Further

Draw a flower for a friend. Give your friend directions on how to color the flower.

BASIC SKILLS

Draw With Directions

Directions: Follow the directions to complete the picture.

1. Draw a smiling yellow face on the sun.

2. Color the fish **blue**. Draw two more **blue** fish in the water.

3. Draw a **brown** bird under the cloud. Draw **blue** raindrops under the cloud.

4. Color the boat **red**. Color one sail **pink**. Color the other sail **green**.

5. Color the starfish orange. Draw two more orange starfish.

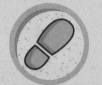

One Step Further

Tell a story about a day at the beach.
Make up characters for your story.

Directions for Decorating

Directions: Follow the directions to decorate the bedroom.

Draw a **red** 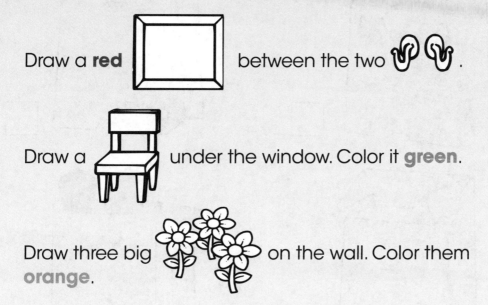 between the two 🪝🪝 .

Draw a 🪑 under the window. Color it **green**.

Draw three big 🌼 on the wall. Color them **orange**.

Draw a picture of something you would like to have in your bedroom.

One Step Further

How is your room decorated?
How would you like to decorate your room?

First Grade Essentials

Following Directions

Follow the directions to make a paper sack puppet.

Directions: Find a small sack that fits your hand. Cut out teeth from colored paper. Glue them on the sack. Cut out ears. Glue them on the sack. Cut out eyes, a nose, and a tongue. Glue them all on.

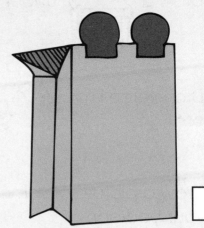

Directions: Number the pictures **1**, **2**, **3**, and **4** to show the correct order.

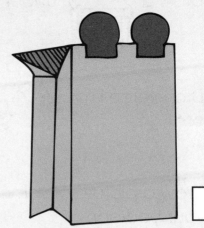

One Step Further

Make a paper sack puppet with a friend.
Put on a puppet show!

Draw a Tiger

Directions: Follow directions to complete the picture of the tiger.

1. Draw **black** stripes on the tiger's body and tail.
2. Color the tiger's tongue **red**.
3. Draw claws on the feet.
4. Draw a **black** nose and two **black** eyes on the tiger's face.
5. Color the rest of the tiger orange.
6. Draw tall, green grass for the tiger to sleep in.

BASIC SKILLS

One Step Further
What is your favorite animal?
What steps do you take to draw this animal?

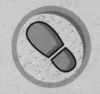

Days of the Week

The days of the week begin with capital letters.

Directions: Write the days of the week in the spaces below. Put them in order. Be sure to start with capital letters.

Tuesday

Saturday

Monday

Friday

Thursday

Sunday

Wednesday

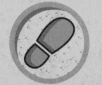

One Step Further

What is your favorite day of the week?
What do you like about it?

Months of the Year

The months of the year begin with capital letters.

Directions: Write the months of the year in order on the calendar below. Be sure to start with capital letters.

January	December	April	May
October	June	September	February
July	March	November	August

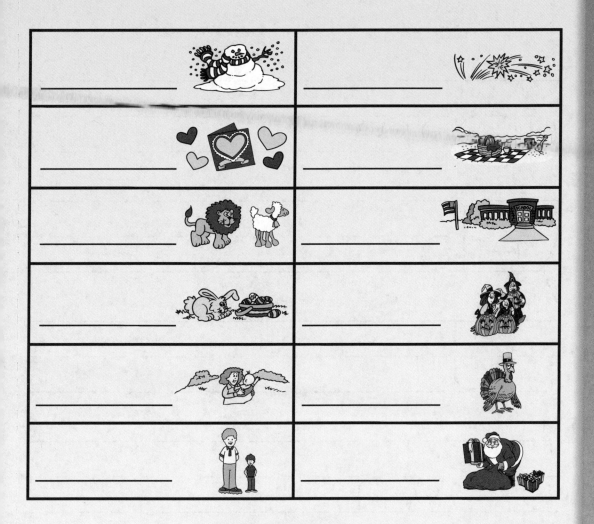

One Step Further

What month were you born in? Do you know anyone else born in that month?

First Grade Essentials

Color Names

Directions: Trace the letters to write the name of each color. Then, write the name again by yourself.

Example:

orange orange

blue

green

yellow

red

brown

One Step Further

Find an object in your home that matches each color on this page.

Number Words

Directions: Trace the letters to write the name of each number. Then, color the number pictures.

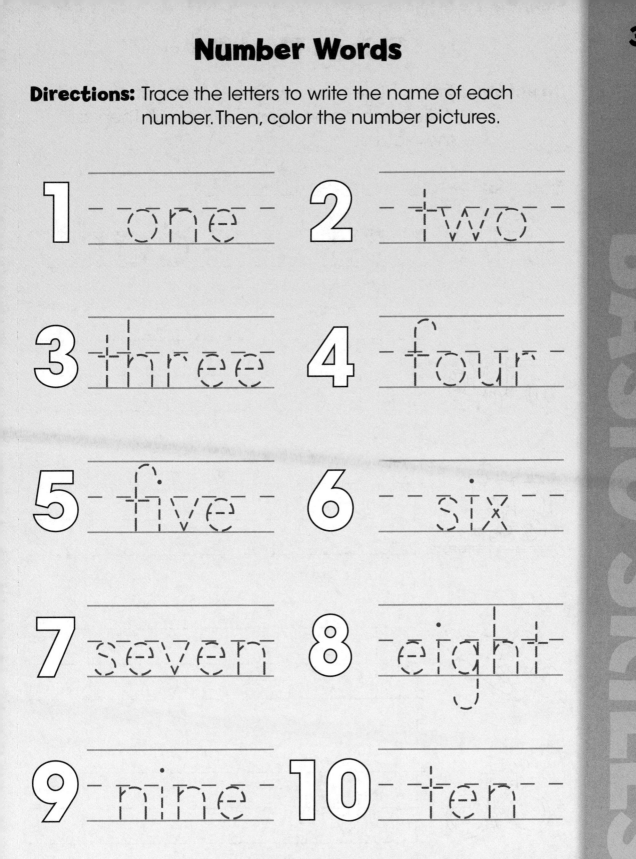

1 one
2 two
3 three
4 four
5 five
6 six
7 seven
8 eight
9 nine
10 ten

BASIC SKILLS

One Step Further
How old are you? Circle that number.
Draw a birthday cake with candles.

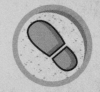

Things That Go

Directions: Trace the letters to write the name of each thing. Write each name again by yourself. Then, color the pictures.

Example:

car   car

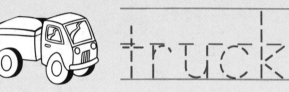

truck

train

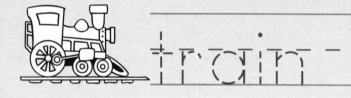

plane

bike

One Step Further

How many of these things have you ridden on? What is your favorite way to travel?

Food Names

Directions: Trace the letters to write the name of each food. Write each name again by yourself. Then, color the pictures.

Example:

bread bread

cookie

apple

cake

egg

milk

One Step Further
Which of these foods have you eaten most recently? Which is your favorite?

Riddles

Directions: Draw a line from the riddle to the animal it tells about.

I am very big.
I lived a long,
long time ago.
What am I?

giraffe

My neck is very long.
I eat leaves from trees.
What am I?

rabbit

I have long ears.
I hop very fast.
What am I?

dinosaur

One Step Further

Tell a riddle about another animal.
See if a friend can guess the animal.

Riddles

Directions: Write a word from the box to answer each riddle.

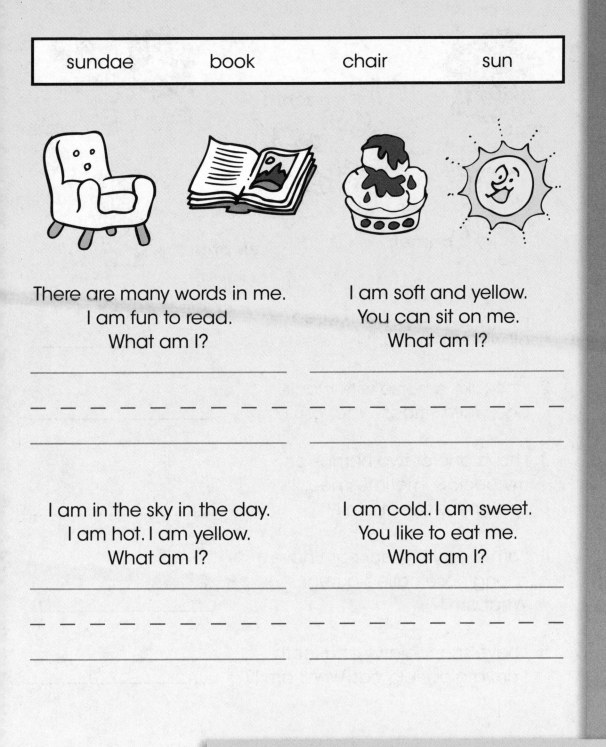

| sundae | book | chair | sun |

There are many words in me.
I am fun to read.
What am I?

_____

- - - - - - - - - - - - - -

_____

I am soft and yellow.
You can sit on me.
What am I?

_____

- - - - - - - - - - - - - -

_____

I am in the sky in the day.
I am hot. I am yellow.
What am I?

_____

- - - - - - - - - - - - - -

_____

I am cold. I am sweet.
You like to eat me.
What am I?

_____

- - - - - - - - - - - - - -

_____

One Step Further
Choose an object at school. Describe the
object and ask a friend to guess.

Zoo Animal Riddles

Directions: Write the name of the animal that answers each riddle.

bear

zebra

lion

camel

elephant

1. I am big and brown. I sleep all winter. What am I? _____

2. I look like a horse with black and white stripes. What am I? _____

3. I have one or two humps on my back. Sometimes people ride on me. What am I? _____

4. I am a very big animal. I have a long nose called a trunk. What am I? _____

5. I have sharp claws and teeth. I am a great big cat. What am I? _____

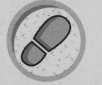

One Step Further

Which one of these animals would you most like to see? Why?

BASIC SKILLS

Reading

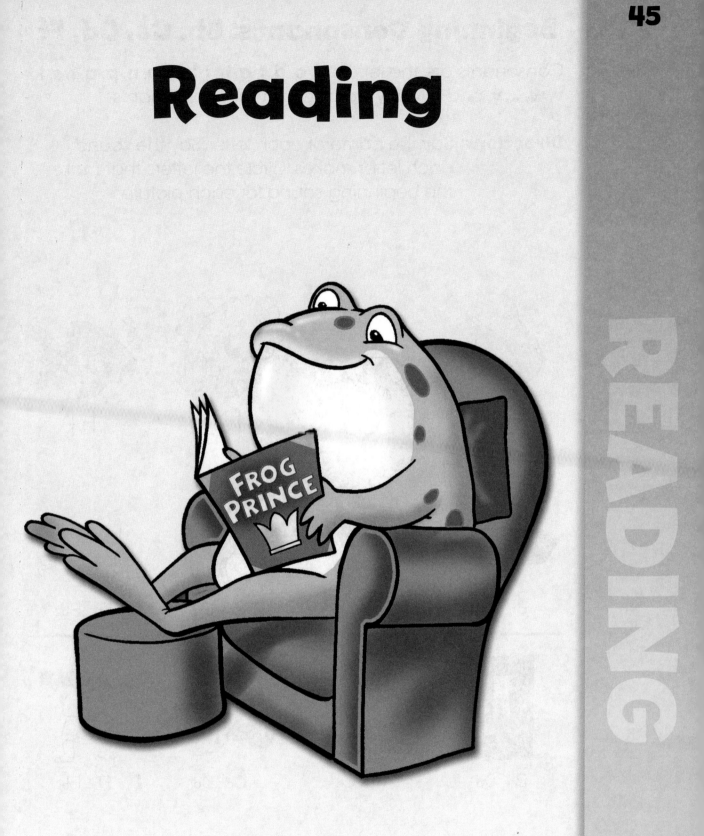

Beginning Consonants: Bb, Cc, Dd, Ff

Consonants are the letters **b**, **c**, **d**, **f**, **g**, **h**, **j**, **k**, **l**, **m**, **n**, **p**, **q**, **r**, **s**, **t**, **v**, **w**, **x**, **y**, and **z**. Many words begin with consonants.

Directions: Say the name of each letter. Say the sound each letter makes. Circle the letters that make the beginning sound for each picture.

Bb   Cc   Dd   Ff

Bb Dd   Ff Cc   Cc Dd   Ff Bb

Bb Dd   Ff Cc   Cc Dd   Ff Bb

One Step Further

Name a friend or family member whose name starts with the **Bb** sound.

Beginning Consonants: Bb, Cc, Dd, Ff

Directions: Say the name of each letter. Say the sound each letter makes. Draw a line from each letter to the picture that begins with that sound.

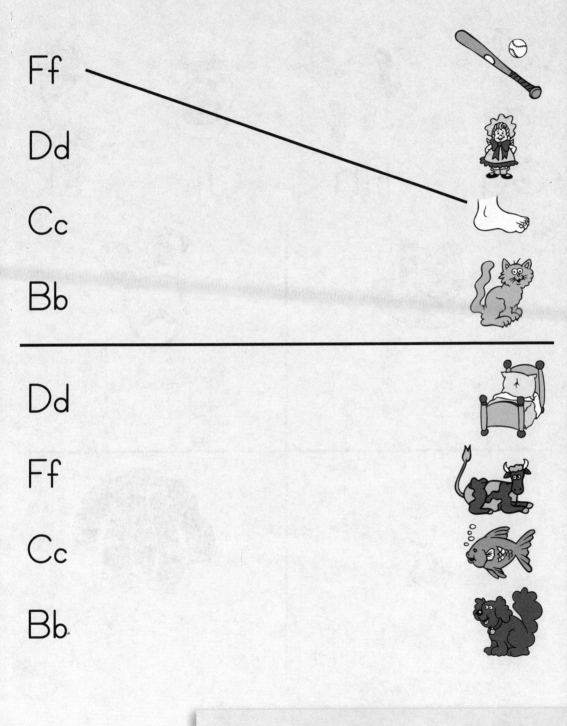

Ff

Dd

Cc

Bb

Dd

Ff

Cc

Bb

One Step Further
Find an object in your home that starts with one of the sounds on this page.

First Grade Essentials

Beginning Consonants: Gg, Hh, Jj, Kk

Directions: Say the name of each letter. Say the sound each letter makes. Trace the letter pair that makes the beginning sound in each picture.

Gg Hh Jj Kk

Kk Hh   Gg Kk

Gg Hh   Jj Gg

One Step Further

Name an animal that starts with the sound of **Gg**, **Hh**, **Jj**, or **Kk**.

Beginning Consonants: Gg, Hh, Jj, Kk

Directions: Say the name of each letter. Say the sound each letter makes. Draw a line from each letter pair to the picture that begins with that sound.

Gg

Kk

Hh

Jj

Kk

Hh

Jj

Gg

One Step Further
Look at a globe. Find a country that starts with one of the sounds on this page.

First Grade Essentials

Beginning Consonants: Ll, Mm, Nn, Pp

Directions: Say the name of each letter. Say the sound each letter makes. Trace the letters. Then, draw a line from each letter pair to the picture that begins with that sound.

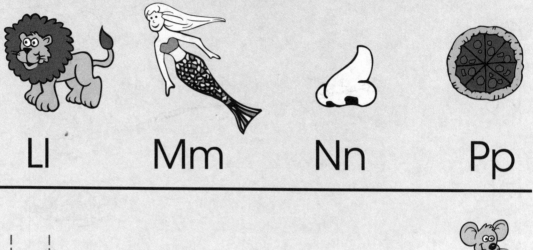

Ll   Mm   Nn   Pp

Ll

Mm

Nn

Pp

One Step Further

Name a state or country that starts with the sound of **Ll**, **Mm**, **Nn**, or **Pp**.

Beginning Consonants: Ll, Mm, Nn, Pp

Directions: Say the name of each letter. Say the sound each letter makes. Trace the letter pair that makes the beginning sound in each picture.

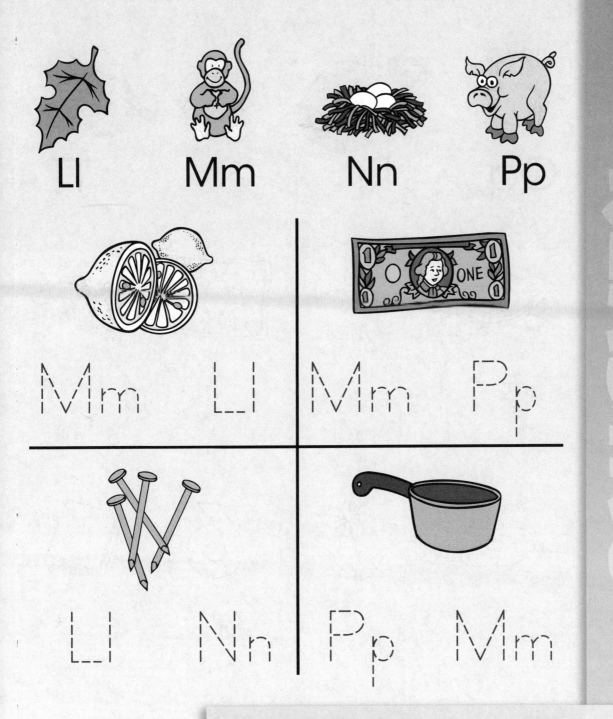

Ll   Mm   Nn   Pp

Mm   Ll   Mm   Pp

Ll   Nn   Pp   Mm

READING

One Step Further
Draw a map of your state. Mark the city where you live in the right spot on the map.

Beginning Consonants: Qq, Rr, Ss, Tt

Directions: Say the name of each letter. Say the sound each letter makes. Trace the letter pair in the boxes. Then, color the picture that begins with that sound.

One Step Further

Name another animal that starts with the **Tt** sound.

Beginning Consonants: Qq, Rr, Ss, Tt

Directions: Say the name of each letter. Say the sound each letter makes. Draw a line from each letter pair to the picture that begins with that sound.

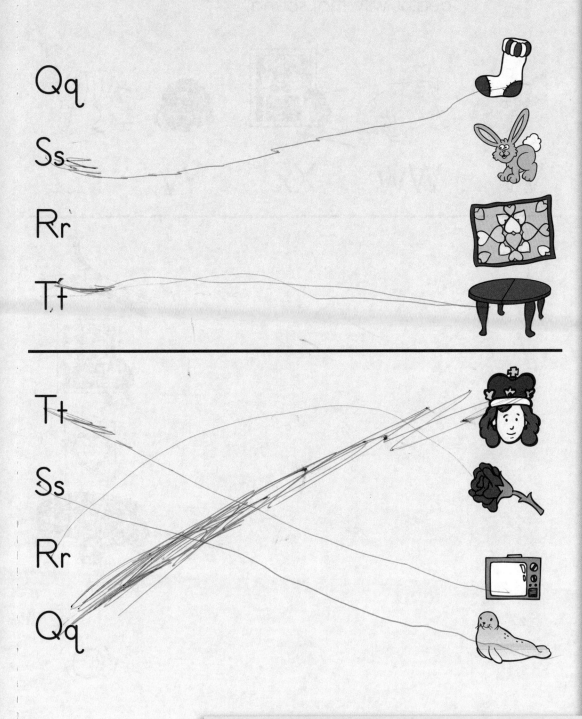

Qq

Ss

Rr

Tt

Tt

Ss

Rr

Qq

One Step Further
Find an object in your school that starts with one of the sounds on this page.

First Grade Essentials

Beginning Consonants: Vv, Ww, Xx, Yy, Zz

Directions: Say the name of each letter. Say the sound each letter makes. Trace the letters. Then, draw a line from each letter pair to the picture that begins with that sound.

Vv   Ww   Xx   Yy   Zz

V v

W w

X x

Y y

Z z

One Step Further

Make a valentine and give it to a friend.
Include words that start with the **Vv** sound.

Beginning Consonants: Vv, Ww, Xx, Yy, Zz

Directions: Say the name of each letter. Say the sound each letter makes. Then, draw a line from each letter pair to the picture that begins with that sound.

Vv

Zz

Xx

Yy

Ww

Vv

Zz

Yy

Ww

Xx

READING

One Step Further
Do you know how to play a musical instrument? What would you like to play?

First Grade Essentials

Ending Consonants: b, d, f

Directions: Say the name of each picture. Then, write the letter that makes the ending sound for each picture.

 ___    ___   ___

 ___    ___   ___

 ___

___   ___   ___

 ___   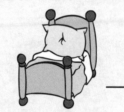 ___   ___

One Step Further
What sound does your first name end with?
What sound does your last name end with?

Ending Consonants: g, m, n

Directions: Say the name of each picture. Draw a line from each letter to the pictures that end with that sound.

g   m   n

g

m

n

One Step Further

Choose an object outside. Say its name. What sound does the word end with?

Ending Consonants: k, l, p

Directions: Trace the letter in each row. Say the name of each picture. Then, color the pictures in each row that end with that sound.

One Step Further

How many of the objects on this page can you find in your home?

Ending Consonants: r, s, t, x

Directions: Say the name of each picture. Then, circle the ending sound for each picture.

r s t x   r s t x

r s t x   r s t x

r s t x   r s t x

r s t x   r s t x

One Step Further
Ask a friend to name several objects.
What is the ending sound for each word?

First Grade Essentials

Make a New Word

Directions: Write the beginning letter of each word in the boxes to make a new word.

1.

2.

3.

4.

5.

One Step Further
Make a list of as many three-letter words as you can. How many did you list?

More New Words

Directions: Write the beginning letter of each word in the boxes to make a new word.

Directions: Write the first letter of each word you wrote to find the mystery word.

___ ___ ___ ___ ___

One Step Further
Name five things you do that make you
happy. Then, go do one of them.

Consonant Blends With r

Sometimes, two consonants at the beginning of a word blend together. Listen for the **dr** blend in **dragon**. **Gr**, **fr**, **cr**, **tr**, **br**, and **pr** are also **r** blends.

dragon

Directions: Draw a line from each consonant blend to the picture whose name begins with the same sound.

dr

br   **cr**

tr

pr   **gr**

fr

One Step Further
Crayon contains a consonant blend with **r**.
Can you name another word?

Consonant Blends With l

Listen for the **cl** blend in **clown**. **Gl**, **pl**, **fl**, and **bl** are also **l** blends.

Directions: Look at the **l** blend at the beginning of each row. Color the picture whose name begins with that sound.

clown

bl

cl

fl

gl

pl

READING

One Step Further
Clap contains a consonant blend with **l**.
Clap your hands 10 times.

Consonant Blends With s

Listen for the **sk** blend in **skunk**. **Sm**, **st**, **sp**, **sw**, **sc**, **squ**, **sl**, and **sn** are also **s** blends.

Directions: Say the name of each picture. Circle the **s** blend you hear at the beginning of the name.

skunk

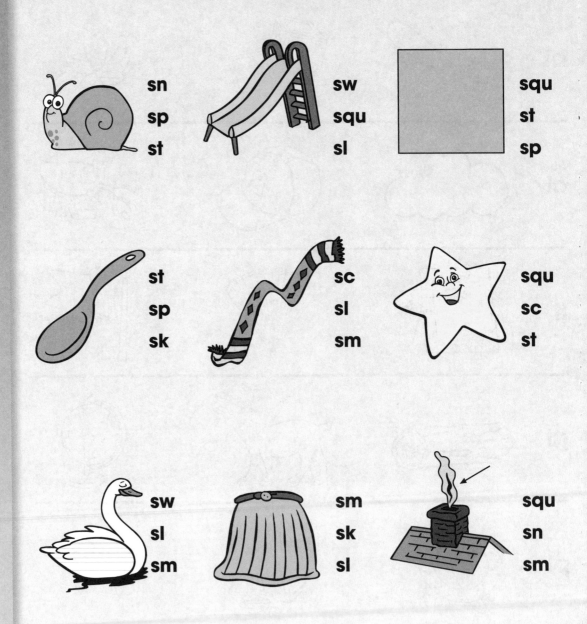

sn
sp
st

sw
squ
sl

squ
st
sp

st
sp
sk

sc
sl
sm

squ
sc
st

sw
sl
sm

sm
sk
sl

squ
sn
sm

One Step Further

Draw a snake. Draw a spoon. What consonant blends do those words contain?

Blends at the Ends

Some consonant blends come at the ends of words. Listen for the **nd** blend at the end of the word **round**. **Mp**, **ng**, **nt**, **sk**, **nk**, and **st** can also be ending blends.

Directions: Say the name of each picture. Circle the blend you hear at the end of the name.

 rou**nd**

nd
st
sk

nt
nk
ng

nt
st
nd

nd
ng
mp

ng
nt
nd

nd
nk
st

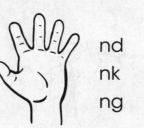
st
nt
nd

nd
nk
ng

nt
sk
st

One Step Further
Be very quiet and listen closely. What sounds can you hear around you?

First Grade Essentials

Meet Short a

Listen for the sound of short **a** in **van**.

Directions: Trace the letter. Write it on the line.

van

A

a

Directions: Color the pictures whose names have the short **a** sound.

One Step Further

How many words can you name that rhyme
with **cat**? Do they have the short **a** sound?

Short a Maze

Directions: Help the cat get to the bag. Connect all the pictures whose names have the short **a** sound from the cat to the bag.

READING

One Step Further

Draw more objects that have the short **a** sound.

First Grade Essentials

Meet Short e

Listen for the sound of short **e** in **hen**.

hen

Directions: Trace the letter. Write it on the line.

Directions: Color the pictures whose names have the short **e** sound.

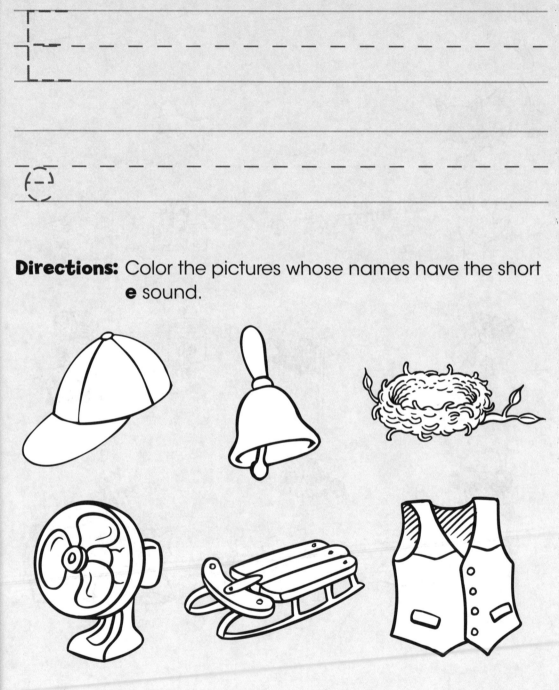

One Step Further

Tell a story about a hen. What words in your story have the short **e** sound?

READING

A Matching Game

Directions: Draw a line to connect each picture with its matching short **e** word.

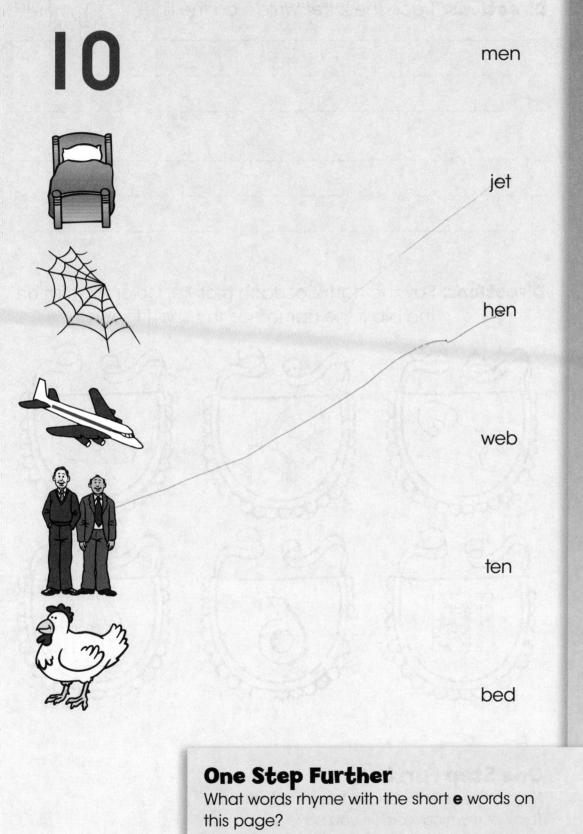

men

jet

hen

web

ten

bed

READING

One Step Further

What words rhyme with the short **e** words on this page?

Meet Short i

Listen for the sound of short **i** in **pig**.

Directions: Trace the letter. Write it on the line.

 pig

Directions: Say the name of each picture. Color the trim on the bib if the name has the short **i** sound.

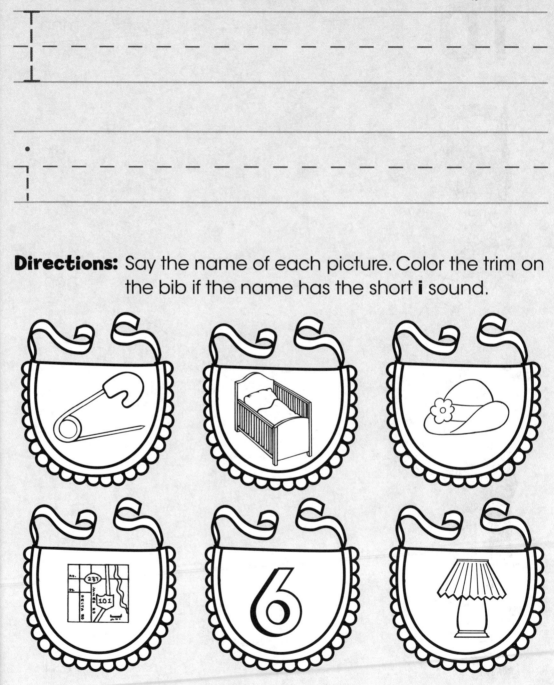

One Step Further

Name six words that have the short **i** sound.
Think of rhyming words if you have to.

Read and Color Short i

Directions: Say the name of each thing in the picture.
Color the pictures whose names have the short
i sound. The words in the box will give you hints.

milk	crib	bib
pig	kitten	fish

One Step Further
Tell a story about what is happening in
the picture.

First Grade Essentials

Meet Short o

Listen for the sound of short **o** in **fox**.

Directions: Trace the letter. Write it on the line.

fox

Directions: Say the name of each picture. Write **o** under the picture if the name has the short **o** sound.

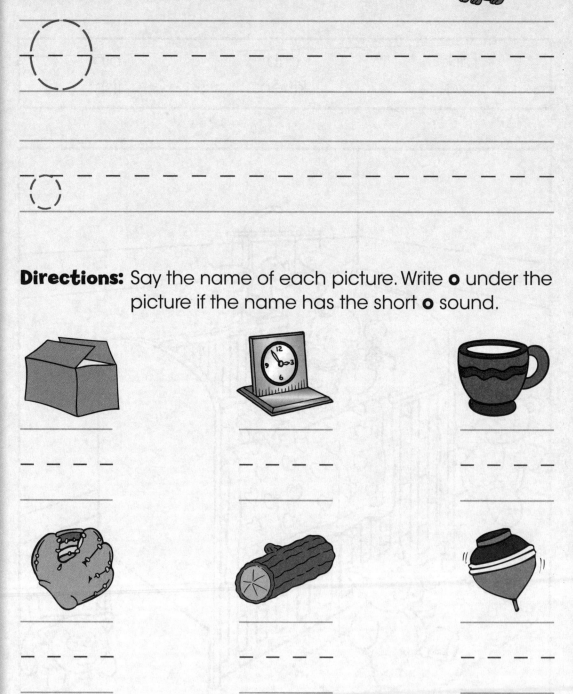

One Step Further

Look around your home for objects with the short **o** sound and put them in a box.

Find Short o Words

Directions: Draw a line under each picture whose name has the short **o** sound.

Directions: The words that match the underlined pictures above are hidden in this puzzle. Circle the words. They may go **across** or **down**.

```
I   T   L   J   B   Z

M   O   O   C   O   T

O   P   G   U   X   U

P   D   O   G   L   P
```

One Step Further

Create your own word search puzzle using words you've learned in this book.

READING

Meet Short u

Listen for the sound of short **u** in **bug**.

Directions: Trace the letter. Write it on the line.

bug

U - - - - - - - - - - - - -

U - - - - - - - - - - - - -

Directions: Say the name of each picture. Color the sun if you hear the short **u** sound in the name.

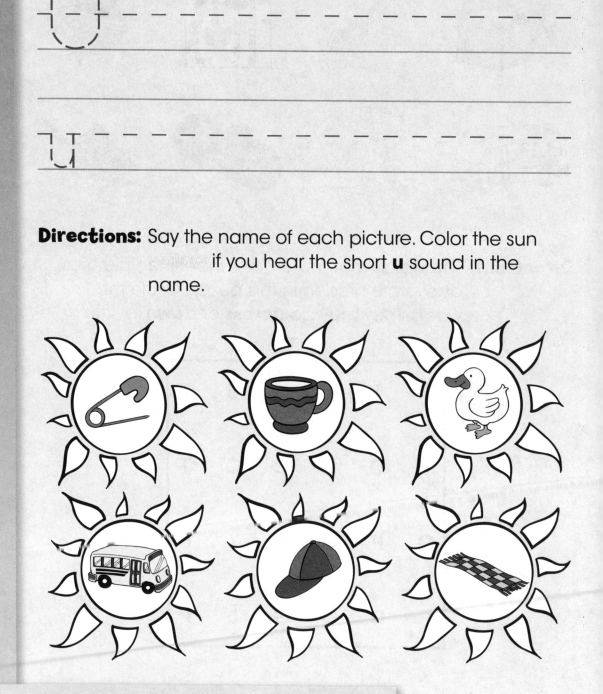

One Step Further
Snug as a bug in a rug! Snuggle under a blanket and read a book.

Short u Tic-Tac-Toe

Directions: Color the pictures whose names have the short **u** sound. Then, play tic-tac-toe. Draw a line through three colored pictures in a row.

One Step Further
Play a game of tic-tac-toe with a friend.
The winner should name a short **u** word.

Meet Long a

Listen for the sound of long **a** in **cake**. Look for **a__e**.

cake

Directions: Color the pictures whose names have the long **a** sound.

One Step Further
What vowels does your name contain?
Are they long or short vowels?

READING

Words With Long a

Directions: Circle the words in the puzzle. The words go across and down.

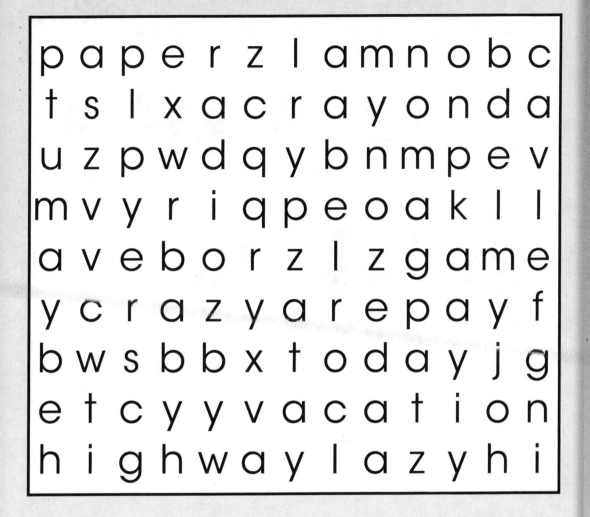

```
p a p e r z l a m n o b c
t s l x a c r a y o n d a
u z p w d q y b n m p e v
m v y r i q p e o a k l l
a v e b o r z l z g a m e
y c r a z y a r e p a y f
b w s b b x t o d a y j g
e t c y y v a c a t i o n
h i g h w a y l a z y h i
```

paper   crayon
radio   maybe
crazy   today
baby   game
lazy   highway
vacation   repay

One Step Further
Draw more objects that have the long **a** sound.

First Grade Essentials

Meet Long e

Listen for the sound of long **e** in **bee**. The letters **ee** and **ea** usually stand for the long **e** sound.

 b**ee**

Directions: Write the name of the picture on the correct line.

 seal ten beet jeep leaf

 bed  red seat feet

ee	**ea**	**Short Vowel e**

One Step Further

Can you think of other words that contain the long **e** sound?

First Grade Essentials

Words With Long e

Directions: Circle the words in the puzzle. The words go across and down.

```
e a g l e t u r f e x y e
a s o m n v s w i a a v a
s t r e e t k t f s g z t
e r p p e a n u t w r a c
l q q l k j e k e e o b f
p s w e e t e u e r e d e
w h e e l m j l n n e h a
p e a c h i h e a s y i s
o w n b r e a k f f g g t
```

eat   easel   sweet   peach   easy   wheel
eagle   peanut   feast   street   fifteen   knee

One Step Further

Look around your room for objects that have the long **e** sound.

Meet Long i

Listen for the sound of long **i** in **bike**. Look for **i__e**.

Directions: Fill in the circle beside the name of the picture.

bike

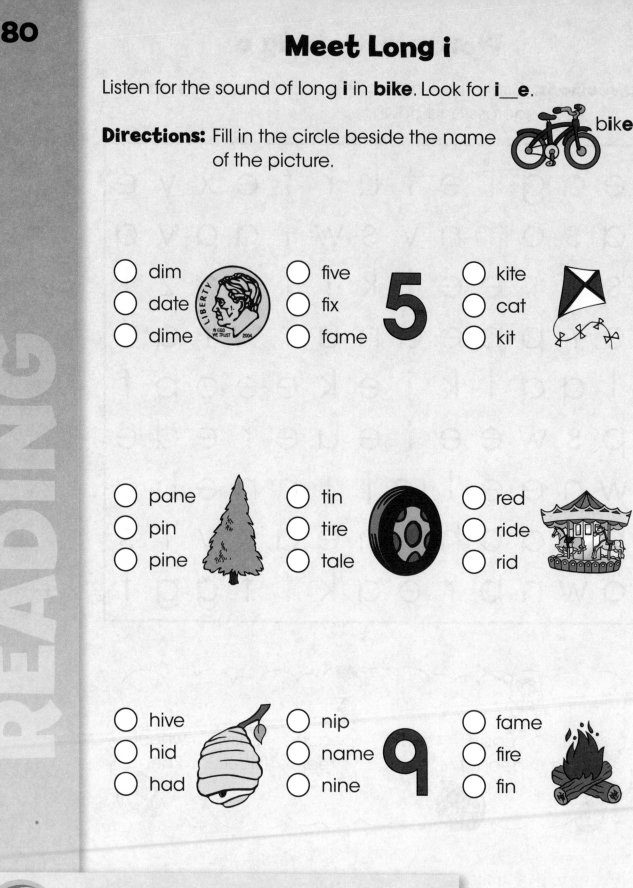

○ dim
○ date
○ dime

○ five
○ fix
○ fame

5

○ kite
○ cat
○ kit

○ pane
○ pin
○ pine

○ tin
○ tire
○ tale

○ red
○ ride
○ rid

○ hive
○ hid
○ had

○ nip
○ name
○ nine

9

○ fame
○ fire
○ fin

One Step Further

What words rhyme with the words you marked? Do they have the long **i** sound, too?

Words With Long i

Directions: Can you find nine hidden pictures of long-**i** words? Circle them.

 bike
 kite
 nine

5 five
lime
pipe

hive
dime
slide

One Step Further

Name the other objects in the picture. What vowel sounds do they contain?

Meet Long o

Listen for the sound of long **o** in **rose**. Look for **o__e**.

rose

Directions: Say the name of each picture. Decide whether the vowel sound you hear is long **o** or short **o**. Fill in the circle beside long **o** or short **o**.

○ Long o
○ Short o

○ Long o
○ Short o

○ Long o
○ Short o

○ Long o
○ Short o

○ Long o
○ Short o

○ Long o
○ Short o

○ Long o
○ Short o

○ Long o
○ Short o

○ Long o
○ Short o

○ Long o
○ Short o

○ Long o
○ Short o

○ Long o
○ Short o

One Step Further

Make up a story. Use at least four of the objects you see on this page.

Words With Long o

Directions: Circle the words in the puzzle. The words go across and down.

```
p v j b r o f e n f k g h
o w u b t r s i o h j l e
e a l o n e q z e r o g r
m x z a p i a n o n m l o
k y p h o n e p o f e o i
e c h o r h o m e g h b d
l p o s g o k e t c y e x
o p e n q s v o l r a n v
m n o c e a n b u z v a w
```

open	no	hero	globe
ocean	zero	echo	alone
poem	piano	home	phone

One Step Further

What do you think makes someone a hero?
Do you have a hero?

First Grade Essentials

Meet Long u

Listen for the sound of long **u** in **mule**. The letters **u__e** and **ue** usually stand for the long **u** sound.

Directions: Circle the pictures whose names have the long **u** sound.

 mule

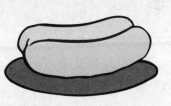
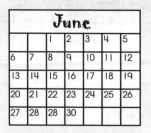

One Step Further

Name your favorite color.
What vowel sound does it contain?

Words With Long u

Directions: Circle the long-**u** word that matches each picture.

cute

rule

tube

dune

mule

prune

dude

glue

Sue

cube

fume

June

blue

tune

flute

rude

One Step Further
Choose a word you circled. Can you name three rhyming words?

Perfect Patterns

Directions: Color the spaces with short-vowel words green.
Color the spaces with long-vowel words orange.

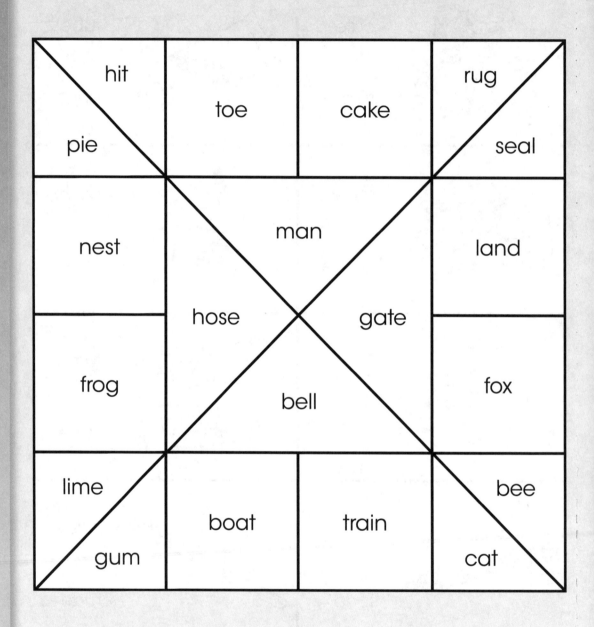

hit / pie	toe	cake	rug / seal
nest	man		land
frog	hose	gate	fox
		bell	
lime / gum	boat	train	bee / cat

One Step Further
What vowels does your name contain? Are
they long or short vowels?

Long and Short

Directions: Color the spaces with long-vowel words **red**. Color the spaces with short-vowel words **orange**.

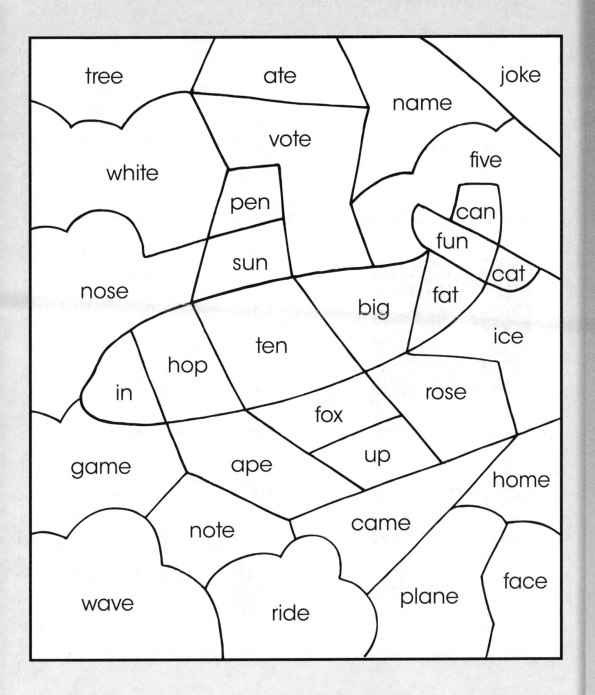

tree

ate

joke

name

vote

five

white

pen

can

fun

cat

sun

nose

big

fat

ten

ice

hop

in

rose

fox

game

ape

up

home

note

came

wave

ride

plane

face

One Step Further

Have you ever traveled by plane? Where would you like to fly to?

Finding Nouns

A **noun** names a person, place, or thing.

Directions: Circle two nouns in each sentence below. The first one is done for you.

The (pig) has a curly (tail).

The hen is sitting on her nest.

A horse is in the barn.

The goat has horns.

The cow has a calf.

The farmer is painting the fence.

One Step Further
Ask a friend to write a sentence.
Circle the nouns in that sentence.

Person, Place, or Thing?

Directions: Write each noun in the correct box below.

girl	school	tree	truck	ball	zoo
artist	park	store	doctor	vase	baby

Person

_____   _____

_____   _____

_____   _____

Place

_____   _____

_____   _____

_____   _____

Thing

_____   _____

_____   _____

_____   _____

One Step Further
What other words could fit into the
Person category?

What Is a Verb?

A **verb** is an action word. A verb tells what a person or thing does.

Example: Jane **reads** a book.

Directions: Circle the verb in each sentence below.

Two tiny dogs dance.

The bear climbs a ladder.

The clown falls down.

A tiger jumps through a ring.

A boy eats popcorn.

A woman swings on a trapeze.

One Step Further
Name the first thing you do in the morning.
What is the verb?

Ready, Set, Go!

An **action word** tells what a person or thing can do.

Example: Fred **kicks** the ball.

Directions: Read the words below. Circle words that tell what the children are doing.

jump
boy

sleep
bed

hello
talk

skate
mittens

hop
sidewalk

sing
song

swim
deep

story
read

READING

One Step Further

Draw a picture of a girl skating in the park.
Go outside and pretend you are skating!

Words That Describe

Directions: Read the words in the box. Choose the word that describes, or tells about, the picture. Write it next to the picture.

| wet | round | funny | soft | sad | tall |

One Step Further

Choose an object in your bedroom.
Use three words to describe it.

Adjectives

Describing words are also called **adjectives**.

Directions: Circle the describing words in the sentences.

1. The juicy apple is on the plate.

2. The furry dog is eating a bone.

3. It was a sunny day.

4. The kitten drinks warm milk.

5. The baby has a loud cry.

READING

One Step Further
Describe your favorite subject in school.
What do you like about it?

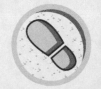

First Grade Essentials

We're the Same!

Words that mean the **same** thing, or close to the same thing, are called **synonyms**.

Directions: Write a word from the word box that has the same meaning as each word below.

bright	hop	dad	fast
pretty	plate	silly	center

sunny

_____

beautiful

_____

middle

_____

dish

_____

quick

_____

jump

_____

goofy

_____

father

_____

One Step Further

Begin your day with a healthy breakfast.
What is a synonym for **begin**?

Words and Meanings

Directions: Read the two words on each dinosaur. If they have the same meaning, color the dinosaur **green**. If they do not have the same meaning, color the dinosaur **red**.

- look
  see
- quick
  speedy
- hot
  cold
- joyful
  happy
- throw
  toss
- tall
  high
- run
  hug
- yell
  shout

READING

One Step Further

Write a sentence. Is there any word in your sentence you can replace with a synonym?

Antonym Artists!

Antonyms are words that have **opposite** meanings. Abby and Abe are Antonym Artists! They like to draw opposite pictures.

Directions: Help Abe draw the opposite of Abby's pictures.

One Step Further

Draw two more pictures that are antonyms.
What did you draw?

Antonyms are Opposites!

Words with **opposite** meanings are called **antonyms**.

Directions: Circle an antonym for the underlined word in each sentence.

1. The sky was very <u>dark</u>.

   purple   old   light

2. Turn <u>left</u> at the light.

   right   sideways   yellow

3. The shelf was very <u>high</u>.

   pretty   low   loud

4. The turtle walked <u>slowly</u>.

   silly   quickly   nicely

5. I <u>whispered</u> at the circus.

   laughed   coughed   shouted

6. Bobby is an <u>adult</u>.

   child   fan   principal

7. The clown was very <u>strong</u>.

   weak   silly   hungry

8. The library is a <u>quiet</u> place.

   fun   messy   noisy

One Step Further

Write a sentence. Ask a friend to write a sentence with the opposite meaning.

READING

Context Clues

Directions: Read each sentence below. Circle the context clues. Choose the answer that fits in each blank. Write it on the line.

1. The cold wind and lack of heat made me wish

   I had an extra _____.
   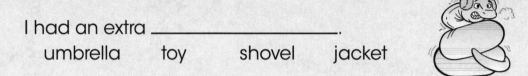

   umbrella   toy   shovel   jacket

2. A whale is a very _____ mammal. Sailors often thought whales were actually small islands!
   small   graceful   large   blue

3. Eating fruit is important for _____ health. Fruit is full of many important vitamins.
   bad   good   okay   cat

4. The bus was very large and had a lot of seats. It could

   carry _____ people.

   few   hungry   many   tired

5. The clown looked very _____ wearing a tiny pink tutu!
   silly   smart   orange   light

One Step Further
Name everything you do for good health.
Do you eat fruit? Exercise?

Context Clues

Directions: Read each sentence below. Circle the context clues. Choose a word from the word list to replace each word in **bold**. Write it on the line.

petted	little	understand	yelled	tell

1. "Don't **reveal** the secret! We want the party to

   be a surprise!" said Mary. _____

2. I can't **grasp** that hard math problem! It is

   too difficult. _____

3. The baby bird was so **tiny** that we could hardly

   see it. _____

4. We **stroked** the soft kitten and heard

   it purr. _____

5. The crowd **hollered** when the player

   was called out. _____

One Step Further

Do something to surprise a friend. Make your
friend a card or give him or her a gift.

Homonyms

Homonyms are words that sound the same, but are spelled differently and have different meanings. For example, **sun** and **son** are homonyms.

Directions: Look at the word. Circle the picture that goes with the word.

1. sun

2. hi

3. ate

4. four

5. buy

6. hear

One Step Further
What was the last thing you ate?
Name eight of your favorite foods.

Homonyms

Directions: Look at each picture. Circle the homonym that is spelled the correct way.

deer   dear

blue   blew

to   two

hi   high

by   bye

new   knew

ate   eight

red   read

READING

One Step Further
What are the last two books you read?
What were the books about?

First Grade Essentials

Batty Bats!

Some words have more than one meaning. The word **bat** has more than one meaning.

Directions: Look at the words and their meanings below. Below each picture, write the number that has the correct meaning.

can: 1. a metal container
2. to know how

_____ _____

band: 1. a group of musicians
2. a strip of material

_____ _____

cap: 1. a soft hat with a visor
2. lid or cover

_____ _____

crow: 1. a large black bird
2. the loud cry of a rooster

_____ _____

One Step Further

Find some cans in your home.
See how high you can stack the cans.

Match That Meaning!

Some words have more than one meaning. Look at the list of words.

Directions: Match the word's correct meaning to the pictures below.

cross: 1. to draw a line through
2. angry

fall: 3. the season between summer and winter
4. to trip or stumble

land: 5. to bring to a stop or rest
6. the ground

_____   _____   _____

_____   _____   _____

READING

One Step Further
Can you name another season that has multiple meanings?

Solve the Mystery

Directions: Read each sentence and cross out the picture. What picture is left?

1. It is not a tube.

2. It is not glue.

3. It is not an ice cube.

4. It is not a mule.

5. It is not June.

6. It is not blue.

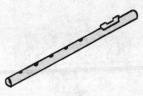

The mystery picture is a _____.

One Step Further

What vowel sound is in all of these picture names? What other words have that sound?

Solve the Mystery

Directions: Read each sentence and cross out the picture. What picture is left?

1. It is not a toy.

2. It is not foil.

3. It is not boil.

4. It is not coins.

5. It is not soil.

6. It is not oil.

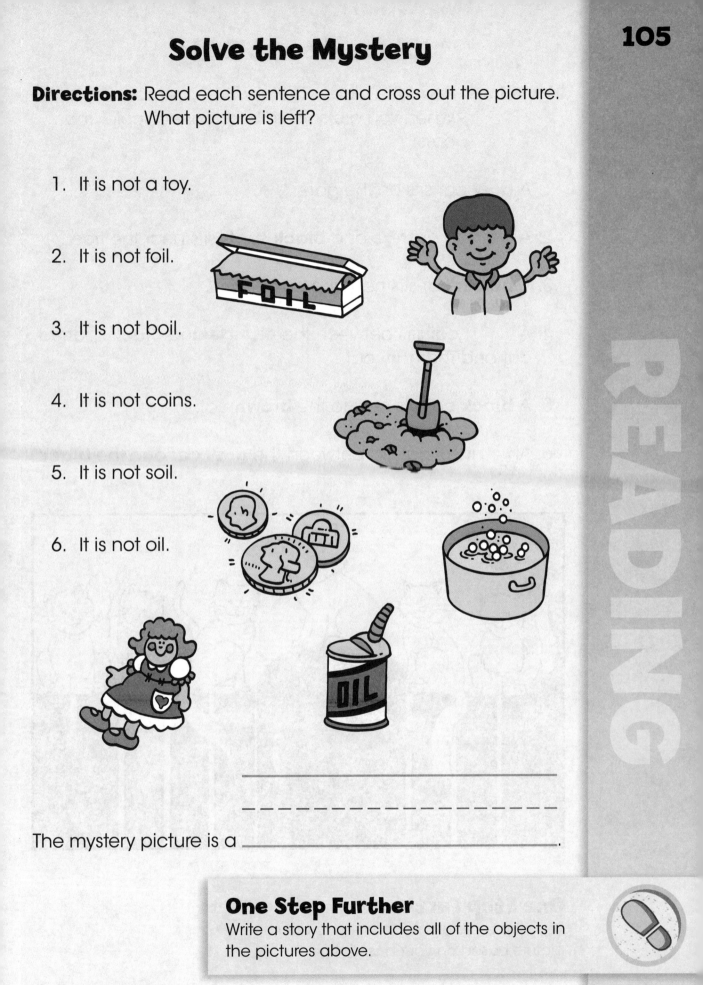

The mystery picture is a _____.

One Step Further
Write a story that includes all of the objects in the pictures above.

READING

Clues About Cats

Directions: Read the clues carefully. Then, number the cats. When you are sure you are correct, color the cats.

1. A **gray** cat sits on the gate.

2. A cat with **orange**-and-**black** spots sits near the tree.

3. A **brown** cat sits near the bush.

4. A **white** cat sits between the **orange**-and-**black** spotted cat and the **gray** cat.

5. A **black** cat sits next to the **brown** cat.

6. An **orange** cat sits between the **gray** cat and the **black** cat.

One Step Further

Describe a picture. Ask a friend to draw the picture based on your description.

Critical Thinking

Directions: Use your reading skills to answer each riddle.
Unscramble the word to check your answer.
Write the correct word on the line.

I am a ruler, but I have two feet, not one.

_____

— — — — — — —

I am a _____.
(ngik)

I am very bright, but that doesn't make me smart.

_____

— — — — — — —

I am the _____.
(uns)

You can turn me around, but I won't get dizzy.

_____

— — — — — —

I am a _____.
(eky)

I can rattle, but I am not a baby's toy.

_____

— — — — — — —

I am a _____.
(nekas)

I will give you milk, but not in a bottle.

_____

— — — — — — —

I am a _____.
(ocw)

I smell, but I have no nose.

_____

— — — — — — —

I am a _____.
(oerflw)

One Step Further
Tell these riddles to a friend.
Did your friend guess the riddles correctly?

In the Community

Directions: Read each story. Circle the better title.

1. Sara and Jenny put on their old clothes. They painted the fence. They swept the walkway. They worked hard.

Helping Out   **Time to Play**

2. The families took their old things to the park. They had a big sale. They gave the money to the Children's Center.

Family Fun   **A Big Sale**

3. Happy Town had a big fair. There were games and rides for the kids. Everyone had a good time!

Fun at the Fair   **Time to Vote**

4. Hill Town wanted its own community center. The people raised money. When they had enough, they built the center.

Our Community Center   **The Big Fire**

One Step Further
Write a short story about what you did today. Give it the best title.

Hey! What's the Big Idea?

Directions: Circle the words that are shown in the picture above.

bowl	pan	scooter	socks
oven	napkins	car	milk
mixer	paper	cat	ink
mitt	towels	dog	phone
spoon	bed	pot	sneakers
spatula	jar	girl	cupcake tin

Directions: Circle and write the best title for the picture.

Baking With Dad   Chocolate Attack!   Eating Food

_____

Tell why the other two titles are not as good.

_____

_____

One Step Further
Ask an adult to help you bake cupcakes.
Describe the steps you take.

READING

Fish Come in Many Colors

Directions: Read about the color of fish. Then, color the fish.

Many fish live in this lake. Fish that live at the top are **blue**, **green**, or **black**. Fish that live down deep are silver or **red**. The colors help the fish hide in the lake.

1. Name three colors of fish that live at the top.

   _____ _____ _____

   _

   _____ _____ _____

2. Name two colors of fish that live down deep.

   _____   _____

   _

   _____   _____

3. Color the top fish and the bottom fish the correct colors.

One Step Further

Is there a fish tank in your home or school?
What color are the fish that live there?

Boats

Directions: Read about boats. Then, answer the questions.

See the boats! They float on water. Some boats have sails. The wind moves the sails. It makes the boats go. Many people name their sailboats. They paint the name on the side of the boat.

1. What makes sailboats move? _____

2. Where do sailboats float? _____

3. What would you name a sailboat? _____

READING

One Step Further
Have you ever been on a boat?
Tell a story about riding on a boat.

Story Time

The **main idea** tells about the **whole story**.

Read the story below.

   "Mom, can we build a fort in the dining room?" John asked.
   "Sure, honey," said John's mom. Then, John's mom covered the dining room table with a giant sheet. "Do you want to eat lunch in our fort?" asked John's mom.
   "Yes!" said John. Then, John's mom brought two peanut butter sandwiches on paper plates and sat under the table, too!
   "Mom, making a fort with you is so much fun!" said John, smiling.

Directions: Does the sentence tell the main idea? Write **yes** or **no**.

1. Then, John's mom covered the dining room table with a

   giant sheet. _____

2. "Do you want to eat lunch in our fort?" asked John's

   mom. _____

3. "Mom, making a fort with you is so much fun!" _____

4. Write a sentence that tells the main idea: _____

   _____

One Step Further
With a friend, build a fort somewhere in your home. What will you do in your fort?

Math

Sums 0 to 3

Directions: Add.

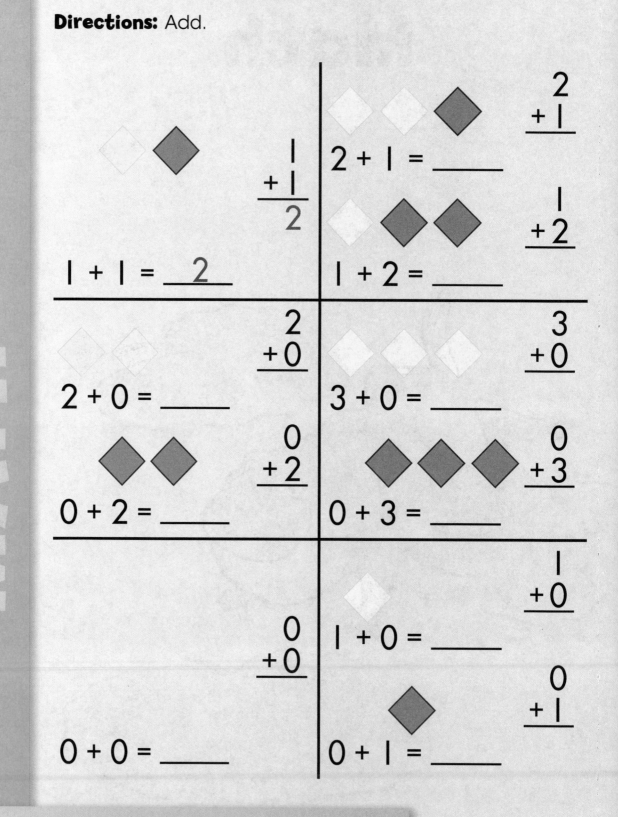

$1 + 1 = \underline{2}$

$\begin{array}{r} 1 \\ + 1 \\ \hline 2 \end{array}$

$2 + 1 = \underline{}$

$\begin{array}{r} 2 \\ + 1 \\ \hline \end{array}$

$1 + 2 = \underline{}$

$\begin{array}{r} 1 \\ + 2 \\ \hline \end{array}$

$2 + 0 = \underline{}$

$\begin{array}{r} 2 \\ + 0 \\ \hline \end{array}$

$3 + 0 = \underline{}$

$\begin{array}{r} 3 \\ + 0 \\ \hline \end{array}$

$0 + 2 = \underline{}$

$\begin{array}{r} 0 \\ + 2 \\ \hline \end{array}$

$0 + 3 = \underline{}$

$\begin{array}{r} 0 \\ + 3 \\ \hline \end{array}$

$0 + 0 = \underline{}$

$\begin{array}{r} 0 \\ + 0 \\ \hline \end{array}$

$1 + 0 = \underline{}$

$\begin{array}{r} 1 \\ + 0 \\ \hline \end{array}$

$0 + 1 = \underline{}$

$\begin{array}{r} 0 \\ + 1 \\ \hline \end{array}$

MATH

One Step Further

Find two pencils. Find one crayon.
Add how many objects there are.

Sums of 4 and 5

Directions: Add.

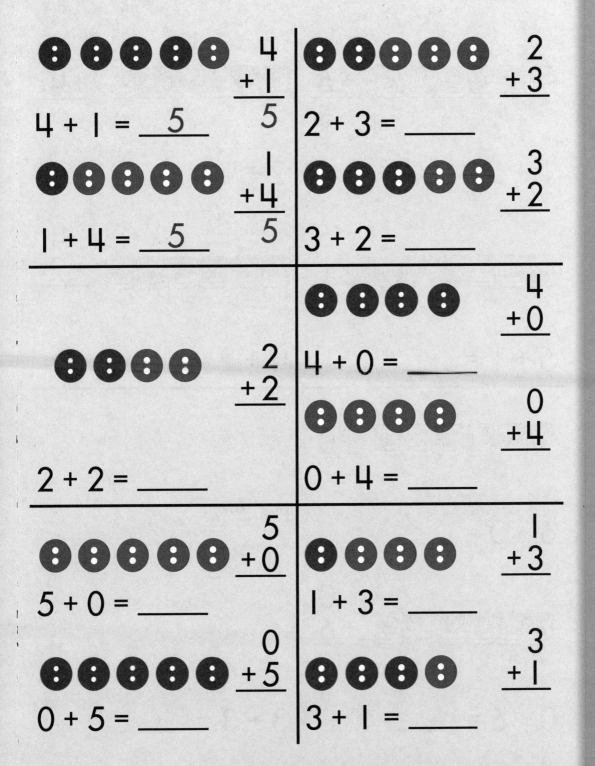

$$4 + 1 = \underline{} 5$$

$$2 + 3 = \underline{}$$

$$1 + 4 = \underline{} 5$$

$$3 + 2 = \underline{}$$

$$2 + 2 = \underline{}$$

$$4 + 0 = \underline{}$$

$$0 + 4 = \underline{}$$

$$5 + 0 = \underline{}$$

$$1 + 3 = \underline{}$$

$$0 + 5 = \underline{}$$

$$3 + 1 = \underline{}$$

MATH

One Step Further
Find four buttons. Find one shirt.
Add how many objects there are.

Sums of 6

Directions: Add.

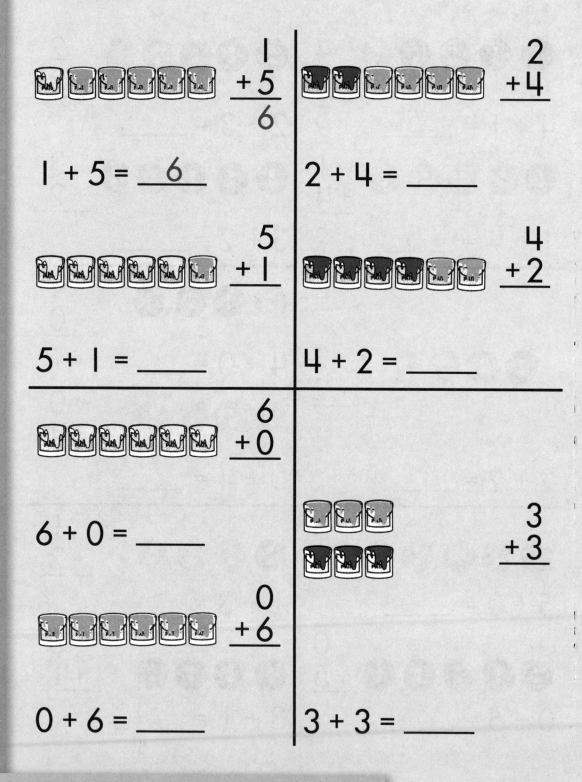

$$\begin{array}{r} 1 \\ + 5 \\ \hline 6 \end{array}$$

$1 + 5 = \underline{6}$

$$\begin{array}{r} 2 \\ + 4 \\ \hline \end{array}$$

$2 + 4 = \underline{}$

$$\begin{array}{r} 5 \\ + 1 \\ \hline \end{array}$$

$5 + 1 = \underline{}$

$$\begin{array}{r} 4 \\ + 2 \\ \hline \end{array}$$

$4 + 2 = \underline{}$

$$\begin{array}{r} 6 \\ + 0 \\ \hline \end{array}$$

$6 + 0 = \underline{}$

$$\begin{array}{r} 3 \\ + 3 \\ \hline \end{array}$$

$$\begin{array}{r} 0 \\ + 6 \\ \hline \end{array}$$

$0 + 6 = \underline{}$

$3 + 3 = \underline{}$

One Step Further

Color a picture using six different colors.
What colors did you use?

Sums of 7

Directions: Add.

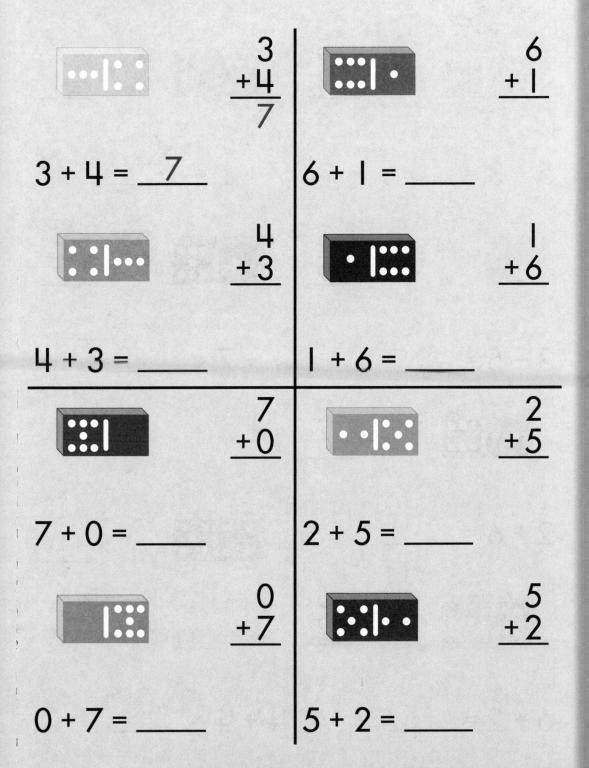

$$\begin{array}{r} 3 \\ +4 \\ \hline 7 \end{array}$$

$$\begin{array}{r} 6 \\ +1 \\ \hline \end{array}$$

$3 + 4 = \underline{7}$

$6 + 1 = \underline{}$

$$\begin{array}{r} 4 \\ +3 \\ \hline \end{array}$$

$$\begin{array}{r} 1 \\ +6 \\ \hline \end{array}$$

$4 + 3 = \underline{}$

$1 + 6 = \underline{}$

$$\begin{array}{r} 7 \\ +0 \\ \hline \end{array}$$

$$\begin{array}{r} 2 \\ +5 \\ \hline \end{array}$$

$7 + 0 = \underline{}$

$2 + 5 = \underline{}$

$$\begin{array}{r} 0 \\ +7 \\ \hline \end{array}$$

$$\begin{array}{r} 5 \\ +2 \\ \hline \end{array}$$

$0 + 7 = \underline{}$

$5 + 2 = \underline{}$

MATH

One Step Further
Roll a die seven times.
What numbers did you roll?

First Grade Essentials

Sums of 8

Directions: Add.

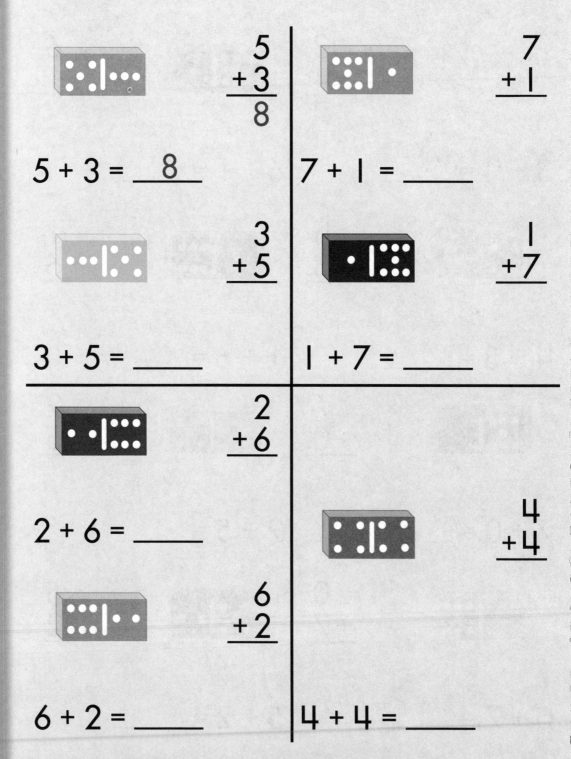

$$\begin{array}{r} 5 \\ +3 \\ \hline 8 \end{array}$$

$5 + 3 = \underline{\quad 8 \quad}$

$$\begin{array}{r} 7 \\ +1 \\ \hline \end{array}$$

$7 + 1 = \underline{\qquad}$

$$\begin{array}{r} 3 \\ +5 \\ \hline \end{array}$$

$3 + 5 = \underline{\qquad}$

$$\begin{array}{r} 1 \\ +7 \\ \hline \end{array}$$

$1 + 7 = \underline{\qquad}$

$$\begin{array}{r} 2 \\ +6 \\ \hline \end{array}$$

$2 + 6 = \underline{\qquad}$

$$\begin{array}{r} 4 \\ +4 \\ \hline \end{array}$$

$$\begin{array}{r} 6 \\ +2 \\ \hline \end{array}$$

$6 + 2 = \underline{\qquad}$

$4 + 4 = \underline{\qquad}$

One Step Further

Find eight small objects. How many different piles of two can you separate them into?

Sums of 9

Directions: Add.

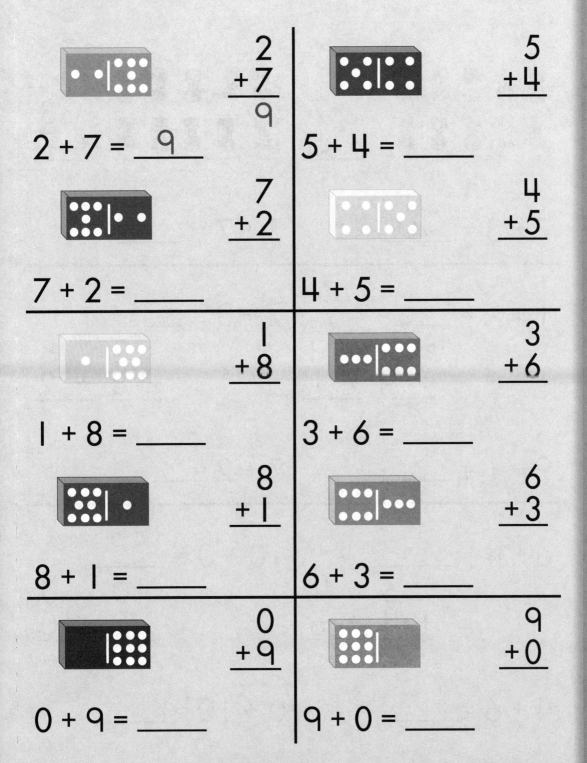

$\begin{array}{r} 2 \\ +7 \\ \hline 9 \end{array}$

$2 + 7 = \underline{\ 9\ }$

$\begin{array}{r} 5 \\ +4 \\ \hline \end{array}$

$5 + 4 = \underline{\qquad}$

$\begin{array}{r} 7 \\ +2 \\ \hline \end{array}$

$7 + 2 = \underline{\qquad}$

$\begin{array}{r} 4 \\ +5 \\ \hline \end{array}$

$4 + 5 = \underline{\qquad}$

$\begin{array}{r} 1 \\ +8 \\ \hline \end{array}$

$1 + 8 = \underline{\qquad}$

$\begin{array}{r} 3 \\ +6 \\ \hline \end{array}$

$3 + 6 = \underline{\qquad}$

$\begin{array}{r} 8 \\ +1 \\ \hline \end{array}$

$8 + 1 = \underline{\qquad}$

$\begin{array}{r} 6 \\ +3 \\ \hline \end{array}$

$6 + 3 = \underline{\qquad}$

$\begin{array}{r} 0 \\ +9 \\ \hline \end{array}$

$0 + 9 = \underline{\qquad}$

$\begin{array}{r} 9 \\ +0 \\ \hline \end{array}$

$9 + 0 = \underline{\qquad}$

MATH

One Step Further

Play a game of dominoes with a friend. What is your favorite game to play with friends?

First Grade Essentials

Sums of 10

Directions: Add.

$$\begin{array}{r} 7 \\ + \ 3 \\ \hline 10 \end{array}$$

7 + 3 = ___10___

$$\begin{array}{r} 3 \\ + \ 7 \\ \hline \end{array}$$

3 + 7 = _____

1 + 9 = _____

$$\begin{array}{r} 1 \\ + \ 9 \\ \hline \end{array} \qquad \begin{array}{r} 9 \\ + \ 1 \\ \hline \end{array}$$

9 + 1 = _____

2 + 8 = _____

$$\begin{array}{r} 2 \\ + \ 8 \\ \hline \end{array} \qquad \begin{array}{r} 8 \\ + \ 2 \\ \hline \end{array}$$

8 + 2 = _____

6 + 4 = _____

$$\begin{array}{r} 6 \\ + \ 4 \\ \hline \end{array} \qquad \begin{array}{r} 4 \\ + \ 6 \\ \hline \end{array}$$

4 + 6 = _____

10 + 0 = _____

$$\begin{array}{r} 10 \\ + \ 0 \\ \hline \end{array} \qquad \begin{array}{r} 0 \\ + 10 \\ \hline \end{array}$$

0 + 10 = _____

One Step Further

Find your favorite book. Read the first 10 lines out loud.

Addition

Directions: Count the shapes and write the numbers below to tell how many in all.

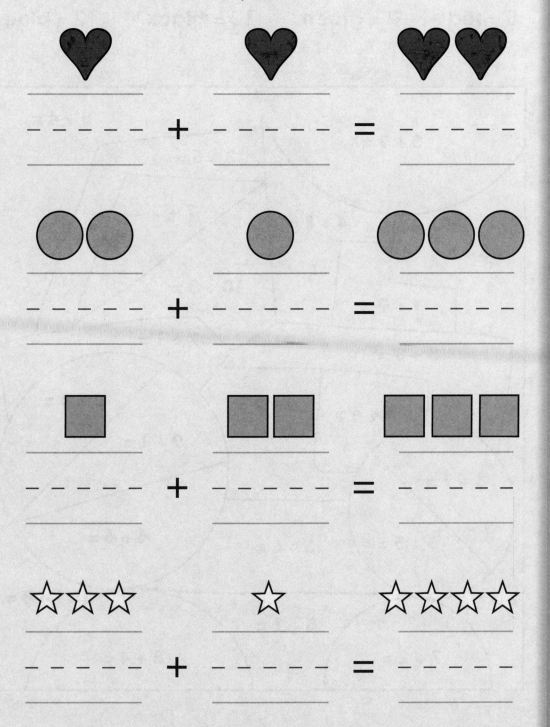

MATH

One Step Further
How many square objects can you find in your bedroom? Count them.

Farmers Need This

Directions: Add. Use the code to color the picture.

8 = **red**   9 = **green**   10 = **black**   12 = **blue**

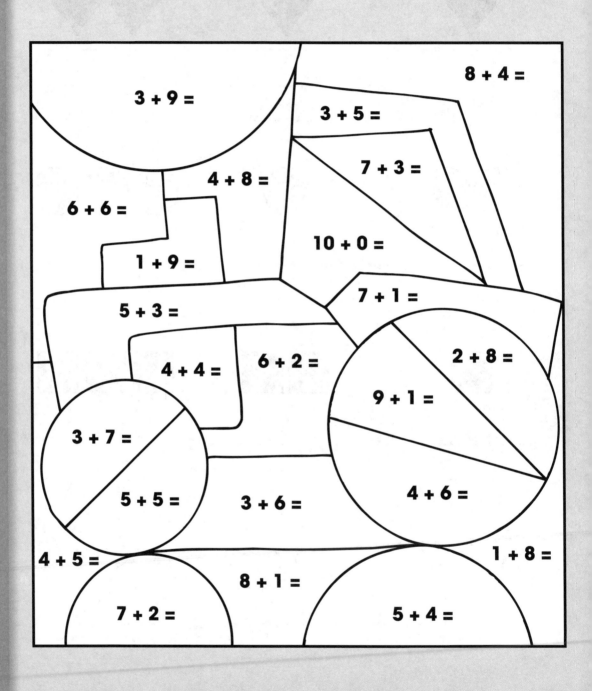

3 + 9 =

8 + 4 =

3 + 5 =

7 + 3 =

4 + 8 =

6 + 6 =

10 + 0 =

1 + 9 =

7 + 1 =

5 + 3 =

2 + 8 =

6 + 2 =

9 + 1 =

4 + 4 =

3 + 7 =

5 + 5 =

3 + 6 =

4 + 6 =

4 + 5 =

1 + 8 =

8 + 1 =

7 + 2 =

5 + 4 =

One Step Further
Tell a story about a day in the life of a farmer.

MATH

What Is It?

Directions: Add. Use the code to color the picture.

6 = yellow   7 = **purple**   8 = **blue**

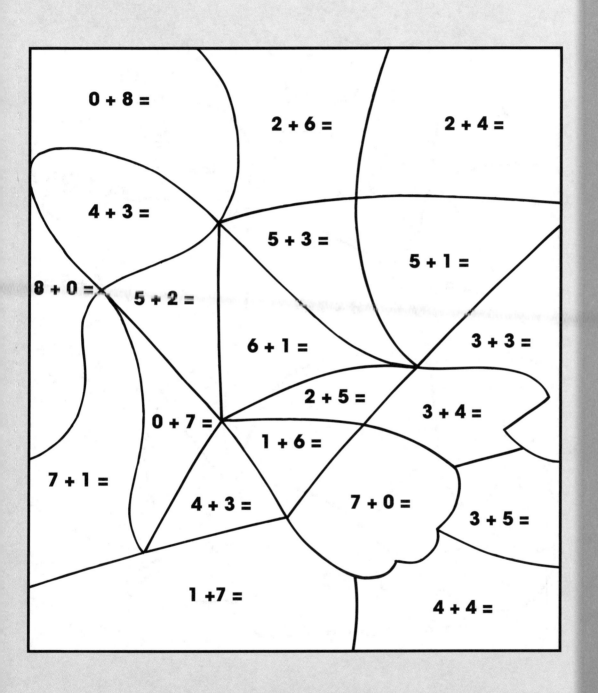

$0 + 8 =$

$2 + 6 =$

$2 + 4 =$

$4 + 3 =$

$5 + 3 =$

$5 + 1 =$

$8 + 0 =$ $5 + 2 =$

$6 + 1 =$

$3 + 3 =$

$2 + 5 =$

$3 + 4 =$

$0 + 7 =$

$1 + 6 =$

$7 + 1 =$

$4 + 3 =$ $7 + 0 =$

$3 + 5 =$

$1 + 7 =$

$4 + 4 =$

MATH

One Step Further

Draw a picture of another object using the colors yellow, purple, and blue.

Watch Out for Me!

Directions: Add. Use the code to color the picture.

8 = **green** 9 = **blue** 10 = **brown**

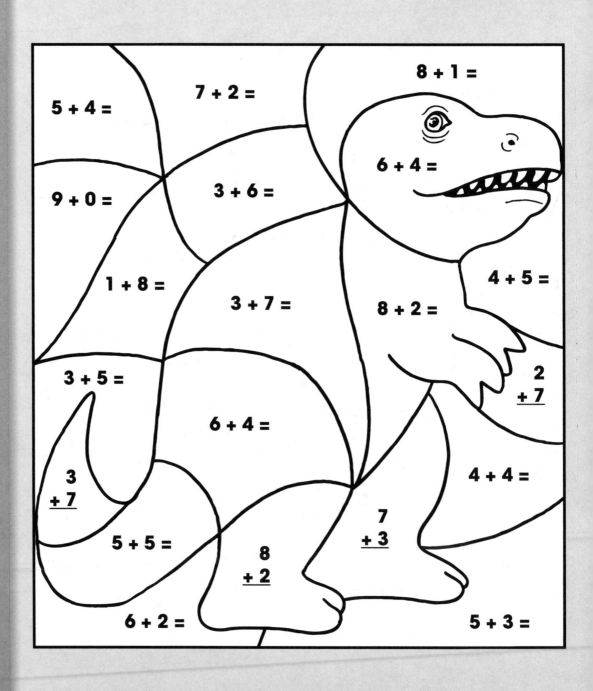

$5 + 4 =$

$7 + 2 =$

$8 + 1 =$

$6 + 4 =$

$9 + 0 =$

$3 + 6 =$

$1 + 8 =$

$3 + 7 =$

$8 + 2 =$

$4 + 5 =$

$3 + 5 =$

$6 + 4 =$

$2 + 7$

$3 + 7$

$4 + 4 =$

$5 + 5 =$

$7 + 3$

$8 + 2$

$6 + 2 =$

$5 + 3 =$

One Step Further

What kind of dinosaur is in the picture? What did that dinosaur eat?

How Many Dinosaurs?

Directions: Count how many dinosaurs. Write the number. Add.

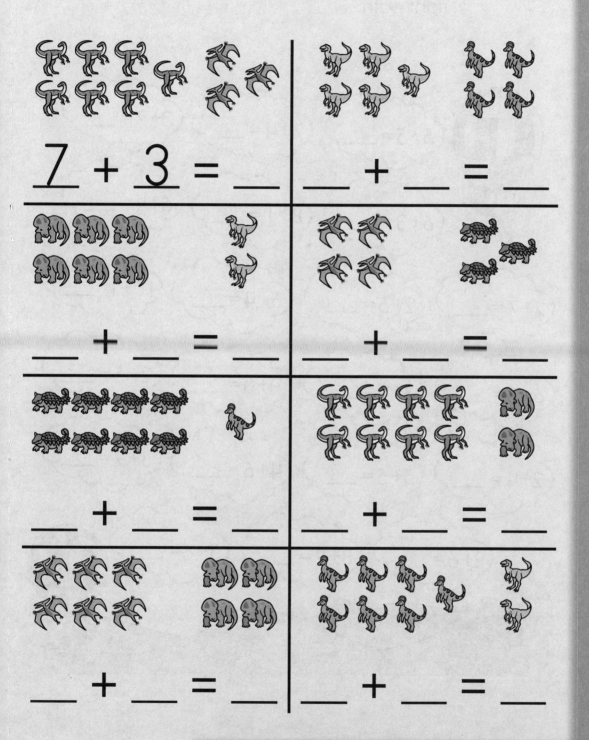

$\underline{7} + \underline{3} = \underline{}$

$\underline{} + \underline{} = \underline{}$

$\underline{} + \underline{} = \underline{}$

$\underline{} + \underline{} = \underline{}$

$\underline{} + \underline{} = \underline{}$

$\underline{} + \underline{} = \underline{}$

$\underline{} + \underline{} = \underline{}$

MATH

One Step Further

Sit outside for a while. How many birds do you see? How many butterflies do you see?

Air Bear Addition

Directions: Help Buddy off the ground. Add to find the sum. Then, color the clouds with sums of 9 to find the right path.

5+5 = ___   7+4 = ___   3+7 = ___

6+3 = ___   8+1 = ___   6+4 = ___

2+7 = ___   2+5 = ___   5+4 = ___   10+1 = ___

6+5 = ___   3+4 = ___   9+0 = ___   2+5 = ___

2+4 = ___   5+5 = ___   4+5 = ___   3+2 = ___

2+6 = ___   8+2 = ___   3+6 = ___

One Step Further

Look up in the sky. How many clouds can you see?

Practicing Addition

Directions: Add.

$$\begin{array}{r} 6 \\ +4 \\ \hline \end{array} \qquad \begin{array}{r} 7 \\ +2 \\ \hline \end{array} \qquad \begin{array}{r} 4 \\ +4 \\ \hline \end{array} \qquad \begin{array}{r} 4 \\ +5 \\ \hline \end{array} \qquad \begin{array}{r} 9 \\ +1 \\ \hline \end{array}$$

$$\begin{array}{r} 2 \\ +7 \\ \hline \end{array} \qquad \begin{array}{r} 6 \\ +2 \\ \hline \end{array} \qquad \begin{array}{r} 9 \\ +0 \\ \hline \end{array} \qquad \begin{array}{r} 2 \\ +5 \\ \hline \end{array} \qquad \begin{array}{r} 1 \\ +4 \\ \hline \end{array}$$

$$\begin{array}{r} 8 \\ +1 \\ \hline \end{array} \qquad \begin{array}{r} 2 \\ +2 \\ \hline \end{array} \qquad \begin{array}{r} 3 \\ +6 \\ \hline \end{array} \qquad \begin{array}{r} 1 \\ +7 \\ \hline \end{array} \qquad \begin{array}{r} 7 \\ +3 \\ \hline \end{array}$$

$$\begin{array}{r} 2 \\ +3 \\ \hline \end{array} \qquad \begin{array}{r} 2 \\ +8 \\ \hline \end{array} \qquad \begin{array}{r} 3 \\ +5 \\ \hline \end{array} \qquad \begin{array}{r} 8 \\ +2 \\ \hline \end{array} \qquad \begin{array}{r} 6 \\ +1 \\ \hline \end{array}$$

$$\begin{array}{r} 1 \\ +9 \\ \hline \end{array} \qquad \begin{array}{r} 6 \\ +3 \\ \hline \end{array} \qquad \begin{array}{r} 3 \\ +4 \\ \hline \end{array} \qquad \begin{array}{r} 5 \\ +2 \\ \hline \end{array} \qquad \begin{array}{r} 5 \\ +4 \\ \hline \end{array}$$

MATH

One Step Further
What two numbers add up to equal your age?

Problem Solving

Directions: Solve each problem.

There are five white ▮ .

There are four blue ▮ .

How many in all?

$$\begin{array}{r} 5 \\ +\ 4 \\ \hline \end{array}$$

There are three ▮ .

Seven more ▮ come.

How many are there now?

Beth has nine ▮ .

She buys one more.

Now how many does she have?

There are six ▮ .

There are three ▮ .

How many in all?

There were eight ▮ .

Two more came.

Then how many were there?

One Step Further

How many T-shirts do you own? How many would you own if you bought one more?

MATH

Plenty to Wear!

Directions: The key words **in all** tell you to add. Circle the key words **in all**. Write a sign in each problem and solve.

1. Jack has four white shirts and two yellow shirts. How many shirts does Jack have in all?

4 ◯ 2 = _____

2. Allison has four pink blouses and six red ones. How many blouses does Allison have in all?

4 ◯ 6 = _____

4. Charley has three pairs of summer pants and eight pairs of winter pants. How many pairs of pants does Charley have in all?

3 ◯ 8 = _____

3. Betsy has two black skirts and seven blue skirts. In all, how many skirts does Betsy have?

2 ◯ 7 = _____

5. Jeff has five knit hats and five cloth hats. How many hats does Jeff have in all?

5 ◯ 5 = _____

MATH

One Step Further
How many shoes do you own?
How many are winter shoes?

Solving Stories

Directions: Write a number sentence to solve each problem.

1. Brad ate five slices of pizza. Todd ate three. How many slices of pizza did both boys eat?

   _____

2. Sam scored four points for the team. Dave scored four points. How many points did Sam and Dave score?

   _____

3. Missy bought six dresses. Dot bought three. How many dresses did they buy in all?

   _____

4. Once there were three bears having a picnic. Then, two more bears joined the fun. Now, how many bears were having a picnic?

   _____

One Step Further

What is your favorite kind of pizza?
How many slices do you like to eat?

MATH

Problems in the Park

Directions: Circle the addition key words **in all**. Write a number sentence to solve each problem.

1. At the park, there are three baseball games and six basketball games being played. How many games are being played in all?

_____

2. In the park, nine parents are pushing their babies in strollers and eight are carrying their babies in baskets. How many parents in all have their babies with them in the park?

_____

3. On one team, there are five boys and three girls. How many team members are there in all?

_____

4. At one time, there were eight men and four boys pitching horseshoes. In all, how many people were pitching horseshoes?

_____

5. While playing basketball, four of the players were wearing gym shoes and six were not. How many basketball players were there in all?

_____

One Step Further

Think of a team you have been on. How many people were on the team?

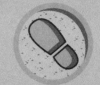

Subtracting from 1, 2, and 3

Directions: Subtract.

$$\begin{array}{r} 3 \\ -1 \\ \hline 2 \end{array}$$

3 − 1 = __2__

$$\begin{array}{r} 2 \\ -1 \\ \hline \end{array}$$

2 − 1 = _____

$$\begin{array}{r} 3 \\ -2 \\ \hline \end{array}$$

3 − 2 = _____

$$\begin{array}{r} 1 \\ -0 \\ \hline \end{array}$$

1 − 0 = _____

$$\begin{array}{r} 3 \\ -0 \\ \hline \end{array}$$

3 − 0 = _____

$$\begin{array}{r} 1 \\ -1 \\ \hline \end{array}$$

1 − 1 = _____

$$\begin{array}{r} 2 \\ -2 \\ \hline \end{array}$$

2 − 2 = _____

$$\begin{array}{r} 3 \\ -3 \\ \hline \end{array}$$

3 − 3 = _____

One Step Further

How many birds can you see out
your window?

Subtracting from 4 and 5

Directions: Subtract.

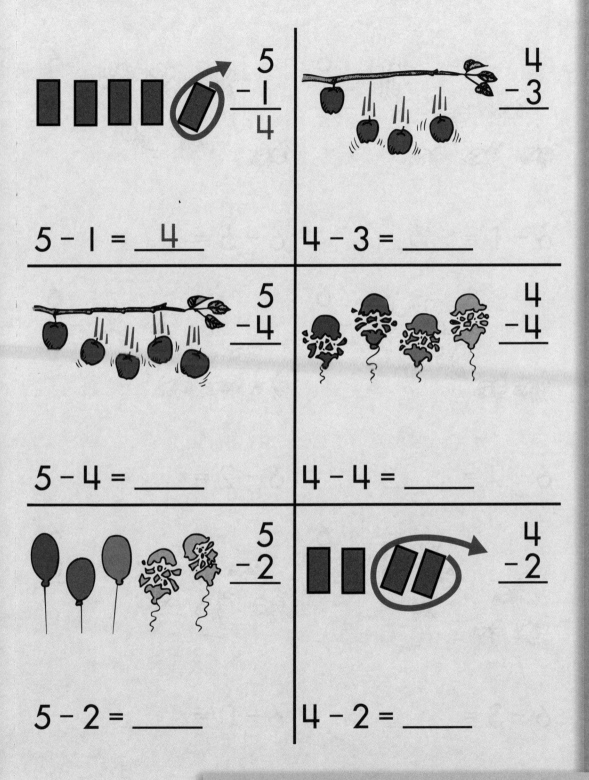

$$\begin{array}{r} 5 \\ -\ 1 \\ \hline 4 \end{array}$$

$$\begin{array}{r} 4 \\ -\ 3 \\ \hline \end{array}$$

$5 - 1 =$ ___4___

$4 - 3 =$ _____

$$\begin{array}{r} 5 \\ -\ 4 \\ \hline \end{array}$$

$$\begin{array}{r} 4 \\ -\ 4 \\ \hline \end{array}$$

$5 - 4 =$ _____

$4 - 4 =$ _____

$$\begin{array}{r} 5 \\ -\ 2 \\ \hline \end{array}$$

$$\begin{array}{r} 4 \\ -\ 2 \\ \hline \end{array}$$

$5 - 2 =$ _____

$4 - 2 =$ _____

MATH

One Step Further
Set up five blocks. Knock two of them over.
How many are left standing?

Subtracting from 6

Directions: Subtract.

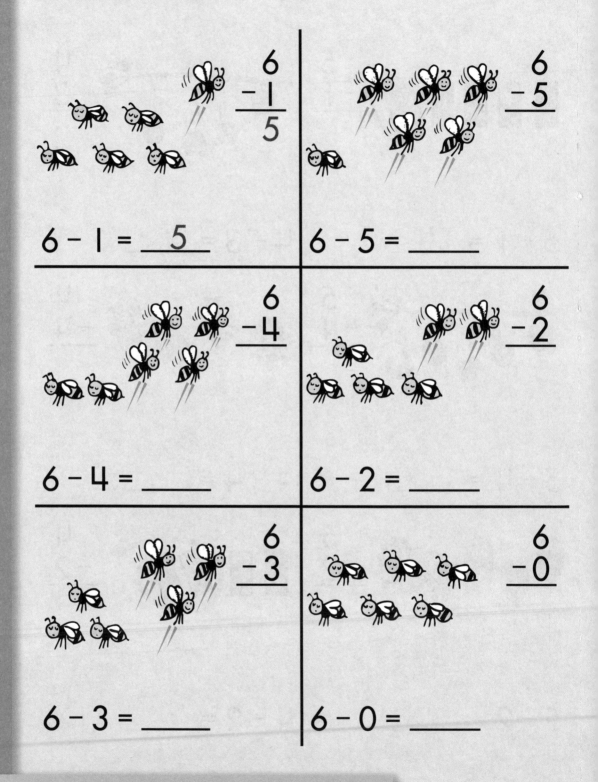

$6 - 1 = \underline{5}$

$6 - 5 = \underline{}$

$6 - 4 = \underline{}$

$6 - 2 = \underline{}$

$6 - 3 = \underline{}$

$6 - 0 = \underline{}$

One Step Further

Draw six flowers for the bees to land on.
Color each flower a different color.

Subtracting from 7

Directions: Subtract.

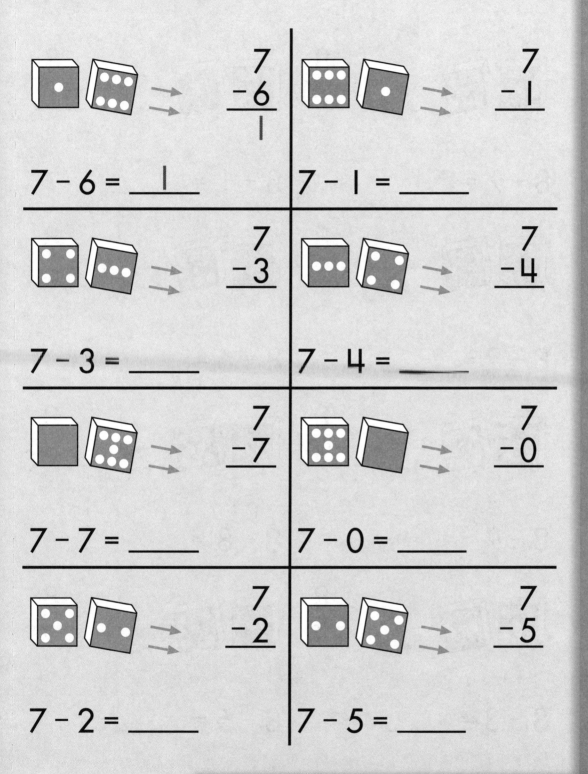

$$7 - 6 = \underline{\quad 1 \quad}$$

$$7 - 1 = \underline{\qquad}$$

$$7 - 3 = \underline{\qquad}$$

$$7 - 4 = \underline{\qquad}$$

$$7 - 7 = \underline{\qquad}$$

$$7 - 0 = \underline{\qquad}$$

$$7 - 2 = \underline{\qquad}$$

$$7 - 5 = \underline{\qquad}$$

MATH

One Step Further
Name the seven days of the week.
What day is your favorite?

Subtracting from 8

Directions: Subtract.

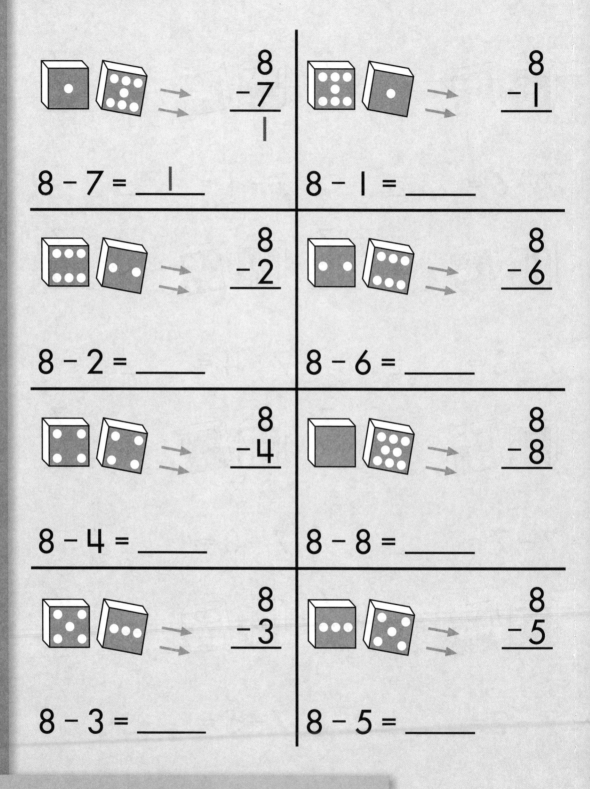

$$\begin{array}{r} 8 \\ -\ 7 \\ \hline 1 \end{array}$$

8 – 7 = ___1___

$$\begin{array}{r} 8 \\ -\ 1 \\ \hline \end{array}$$

8 – 1 = _____

$$\begin{array}{r} 8 \\ -\ 2 \\ \hline \end{array}$$

8 – 2 = _____

$$\begin{array}{r} 8 \\ -\ 6 \\ \hline \end{array}$$

8 – 6 = _____

$$\begin{array}{r} 8 \\ -\ 4 \\ \hline \end{array}$$

8 – 4 = _____

$$\begin{array}{r} 8 \\ -\ 8 \\ \hline \end{array}$$

8 – 8 = _____

$$\begin{array}{r} 8 \\ -\ 3 \\ \hline \end{array}$$

8 – 3 = _____

$$\begin{array}{r} 8 \\ -\ 5 \\ \hline \end{array}$$

8 – 5 = _____

One Step Further
Can you name at least eight states?
What state do you live in?

Subtracting from 9

Directions: Subtract.

$$\begin{array}{r} 9 \\ -6 \\ \hline 3 \end{array}$$

$9 - 6 = \underline{3}$

$$\begin{array}{r} 9 \\ -3 \\ \hline \end{array}$$

$9 - 3 = \underline{}$

$$\begin{array}{r} 9 \\ -0 \\ \hline \end{array}$$

$9 - 0 = \underline{}$

$$\begin{array}{r} 9 \\ -9 \\ \hline \end{array}$$

$9 - 9 = \underline{}$

$$\begin{array}{r} 9 \\ -5 \\ \hline \end{array}$$

$9 - 5 = \underline{}$

$$\begin{array}{r} 9 \\ -4 \\ \hline \end{array}$$

$9 - 4 = \underline{}$

$$\begin{array}{r} 9 \\ -8 \\ \hline \end{array}$$

$9 - 8 = \underline{}$

$$\begin{array}{r} 9 \\ -1 \\ \hline \end{array}$$

$9 - 1 = \underline{}$

MATH

One Step Further
Roll two dice. How many rolls do you make until you roll a total of nine?

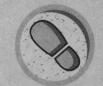

Subtracting from 10

Directions: Subtract.

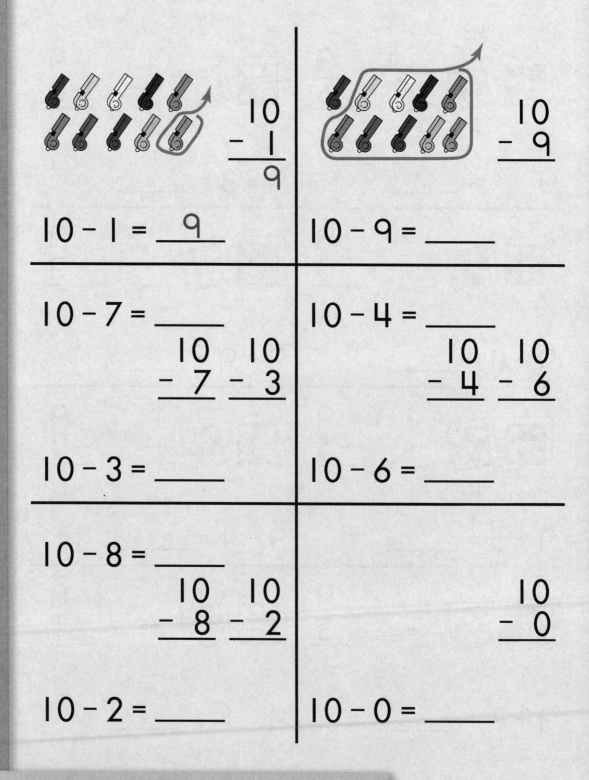

$$\begin{array}{r} 10 \\ -\ 1 \\ \hline 9 \end{array}$$

$$\begin{array}{r} 10 \\ -\ 9 \\ \hline \end{array}$$

10 – 1 = __9__   10 – 9 = _____

10 – 7 = _____   10 – 4 = _____

$$\begin{array}{r} 10 \\ -\ 7 \\ \hline \end{array} \quad \begin{array}{r} 10 \\ -\ 3 \\ \hline \end{array}$$ $$\begin{array}{r} 10 \\ -\ 4 \\ \hline \end{array} \quad \begin{array}{r} 10 \\ -\ 6 \\ \hline \end{array}$$

10 – 3 = _____   10 – 6 = _____

10 – 8 = _____

$$\begin{array}{r} 10 \\ -\ 8 \\ \hline \end{array} \quad \begin{array}{r} 10 \\ -\ 2 \\ \hline \end{array}$$ $$\begin{array}{r} 10 \\ -\ 0 \\ \hline \end{array}$$

10 – 2 = _____   10 – 0 = _____

One Step Further
Can you whistle? Try to whistle for 10 seconds while standing on one foot.

A Swinging Adventure

Directions: Solve the subtraction problems.

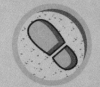

$$\begin{array}{r} 7 \\ -\ 2 \\ \hline \end{array} \qquad \begin{array}{r} 6 \\ -\ 3 \\ \hline \end{array} \qquad \begin{array}{r} 4 \\ -\ 3 \\ \hline \end{array} \qquad \begin{array}{r} 3 \\ -\ 2 \\ \hline \end{array}$$

$$\begin{array}{r} 10 \\ -\ 7 \\ \hline \end{array} \qquad \begin{array}{r} 7 \\ -\ 1 \\ \hline \end{array} \qquad \begin{array}{r} 10 \\ -\ 1 \\ \hline \end{array} \qquad \begin{array}{r} 7 \\ -\ 4 \\ \hline \end{array}$$

$$\begin{array}{r} 6 \\ -\ 4 \\ \hline \end{array} \qquad \begin{array}{r} 8 \\ -\ 4 \\ \hline \end{array} \qquad \begin{array}{r} 9 \\ -\ 5 \\ \hline \end{array} \qquad \begin{array}{r} 8 \\ -\ 1 \\ \hline \end{array} \qquad \begin{array}{r} 9 \\ -\ 2 \\ \hline \end{array}$$

$$\begin{array}{r} 9 \\ -\ 6 \\ \hline \end{array} \qquad \begin{array}{r} 5 \\ -\ 4 \\ \hline \end{array} \qquad \begin{array}{r} 10 \\ -\ 6 \\ \hline \end{array} \qquad \begin{array}{r} 7 \\ -\ 3 \\ \hline \end{array} \qquad \begin{array}{r} 4 \\ -\ 2 \\ \hline \end{array}$$

$$\begin{array}{r} 5 \\ -\ 1 \\ \hline \end{array} \qquad \begin{array}{r} 9 \\ -\ 5 \\ \hline \end{array} \qquad \begin{array}{r} 9 \\ -\ 3 \\ \hline \end{array} \qquad \begin{array}{r} 8 \\ -\ 5 \\ \hline \end{array} \qquad \begin{array}{r} 7 \\ -\ 3 \\ \hline \end{array}$$

MATH

One Step Further
Get with a friend and put on a play about Robin Hood.

Subtracting

Six silly green frogs were sitting on six lily pads.

A big bird flew by and two frogs jumped off into the water.

MATH

Directions: Solve the subtraction problem by answering the questions.

How many frogs were sitting on the lily pads? _____

How many frogs jumped off? _____

How many frogs were left? _____

One Step Further
Hop like a frog four times. How many birds can you see outside right now?

Subtracting

Four hungry cats went
on a picnic.

Two cats spotted some mice
and took off to catch them!

MATH

Directions: Solve the subtraction problem by answering the
questions.

How many cats went on the picnic? _____

How many cats ran after the mice? _____

How many cats were left? _____

One Step Further

Tell a story about the cats' picnic.
What happened before the mice came?

How Many Left?

Directions: Solve each problem.

$$\begin{array}{r} 10 \\ -\ 4 \\ \hline \end{array}$$

There are 10 white ✿ .

There are four blue .

How many more white ✿ than blue ✿ are there? _____

Ten 🖍 are on the table.

Two are broken.

How many are not broken? _____

There are nine 🐟 .

Six swim away.

How many 🐟 are left? _____

Joni wants nine 🪙 .

She has five 🪙 .

How many more does she need? _____

There were 10 ⛄ .

Five ⛄ melted.

How many did not melt? _____

One Step Further
What color flowers are outside your home?
Draw a picture of your favorite flower.

MATH

How Many Animals Are Left?

Directions: The key word **left** tells you to subtract. Circle the key word **left**. Write a number sentence to solve each subtraction problem.

1. Bill had 10 kittens, but four of them ran away. How many kittens does he have left?

$$10 - 4 = 6$$

2. There were 12 rabbits eating in the garden. Dogs chased three of them away. How many rabbits were left?

_____

3. There were 14 frogs on the bank of the pond. Then, nine of them hopped into the water. How many frogs were left on the bank?

_____

4. Bill saw 11 birds eating from the bird feeders in his backyard. A cat scared seven of them away. How many birds were left at the feeders?

_____

5. Bill counted 15 robins in his yard. Then, eight of the robins flew away. How many robins were left in the yard?

_____

MATH

One Step Further
Is there a bird feeder in your yard?
How many birds are eating from the feeder?

Fish Bowl

Directions: Color **20** fish 🐟. Circle to show how many fish are left over.

5   **6**   **7**

MATH

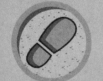

One Step Further

Go to a pet store. How many fish tanks are there? How many fish are in each tank?

Frog Fun

Directions: Color **22** frogs . Circle to show how many frogs are left over.

3   4   5

One Step Further

If there are **22** frogs and **7** lily pads, how many frogs do not have a lily pad to sit on?

MATH

Snail Garden

Directions: Color **25** snails . Circle to show how many snails are left over.

3   4   5

One Step Further
Use three words to describe a snail. Have you ever seen a snail in your yard?

MATH

Working on Webs

Directions: Color **25** spiders . Circle to show how many spiders are left over.

1   2   3

One Step Further

A spider has eight legs. How many legs in all will three spiders have?

Picture Problems

Directions: Solve the number problem under each picture. Write **+** or **−** to show if you should add or subtract.

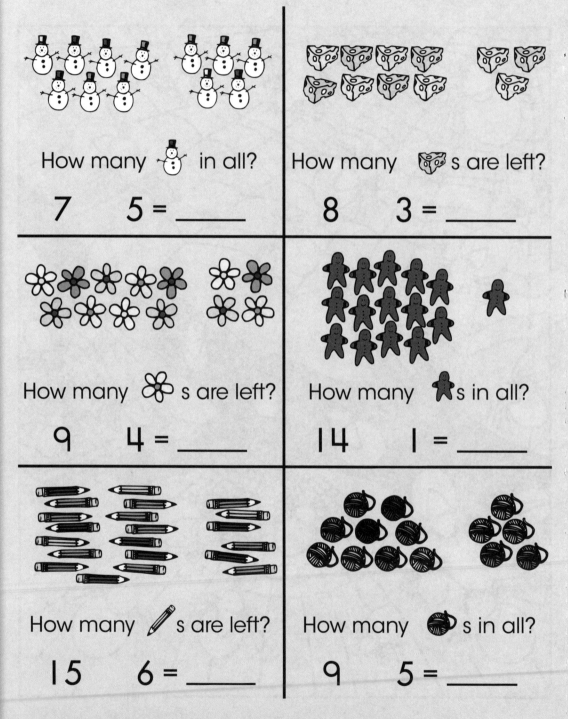

How many 🛷 in all?

7   5 = _____

How many 🧀 s are left?

8   3 = _____

How many 🌼 s are left?

9   4 = _____

How many 🍪 s in all?

14   1 = _____

How many ✏️ s are left?

15   6 = _____

How many 🧶 s in all?

9   5 = _____

One Step Further
Grab some pencils. Take away three of them.
How many are left?

Puppy Problems

Directions: Look at the pictures. Complete the number sentences.

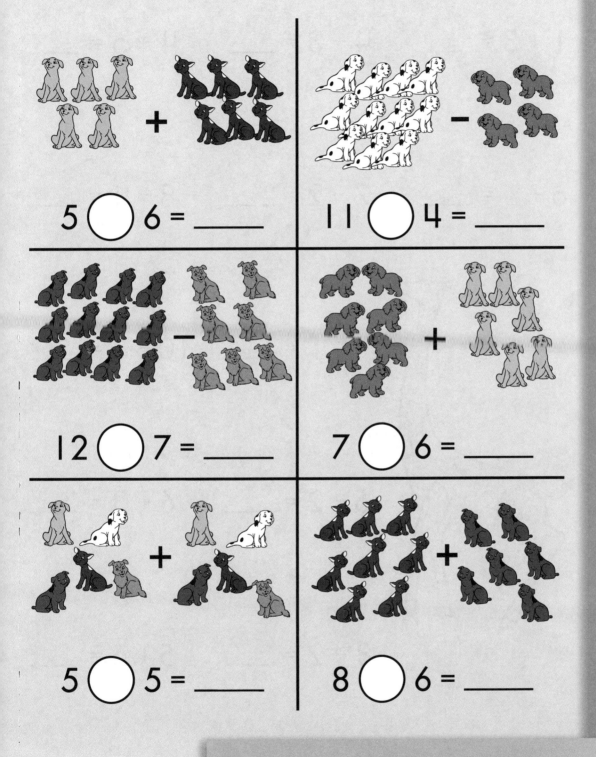

5 ◯ 6 = _____

11 ◯ 4 = _____

12 ◯ 7 = _____

7 ◯ 6 = _____

5 ◯ 5 = _____

8 ◯ 6 = _____

MATH

One Step Further

Name your favorite book or movie about dogs.

First Grade Essentials

Addition and Subtraction

Directions: Solve the problems.

1 + 3 = ____   4 − 3 = ____   4 + 5 = ____

6 + 1 = ____   7 − 2 = ____   8 − 4 = ____

9 − 1 = ____   10 − 3 = ____

5 − 2 = ____   6 + 3 = ____

8 + 2 = ____   5 + 5 = ____

One Step Further

What is your favorite zoo animal?
What do you like about it?

Add or Subtract?

Directions: The key words **in all** tell you to add. The key word **left** tells you to subtract. Circle the key words and write **+** or **−** in the circles. Then, solve the problems.

1. The pet store has three large dogs and five small dogs. How many dogs are there in all?

3  5 = _____

4. The pet store gave Tasha's class two adult gerbils and nine young ones. How many gerbils did Tasha's class get in all?

2 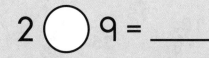 9 = _____

2. The pet store had nine parrots and then sold four of them. How many parrots does the pet store have left?

9 ◯ 4 = _____

3. At the pet store, three of the eight kittens were sold. How many kittens are left in the pet store?

8 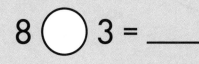 3 = _____

5. The monkey has five rubber toys and four wooden toys. How many toys does the monkey have in all?

5 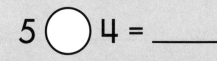 4 = _____

MATH

One Step Further
What pet would you most like to have from a pet store?

Helen the Housefly

Directions: Connect the dots from **0** to **100**. Color the picture.

MATH

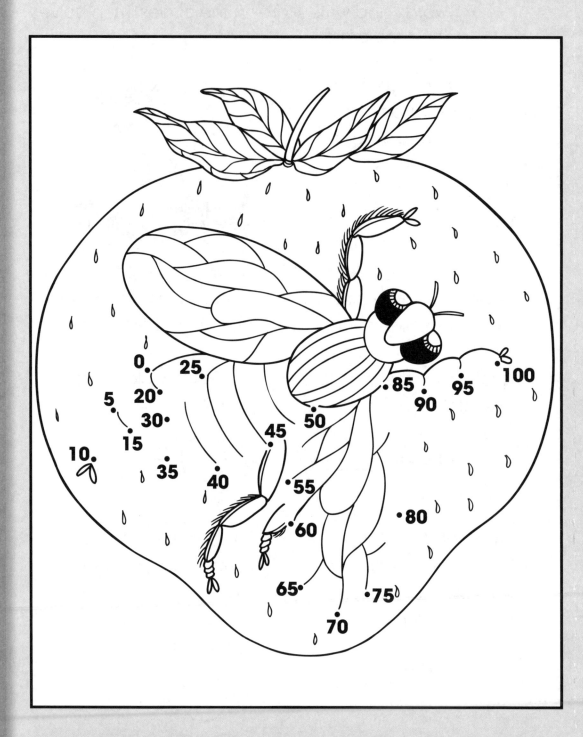

One Step Further

Write a story about why flies buzz in people's ears.

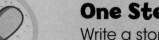

Chris the Cricket

Directions: Connect the dots from **15** to **100**. Color the picture.

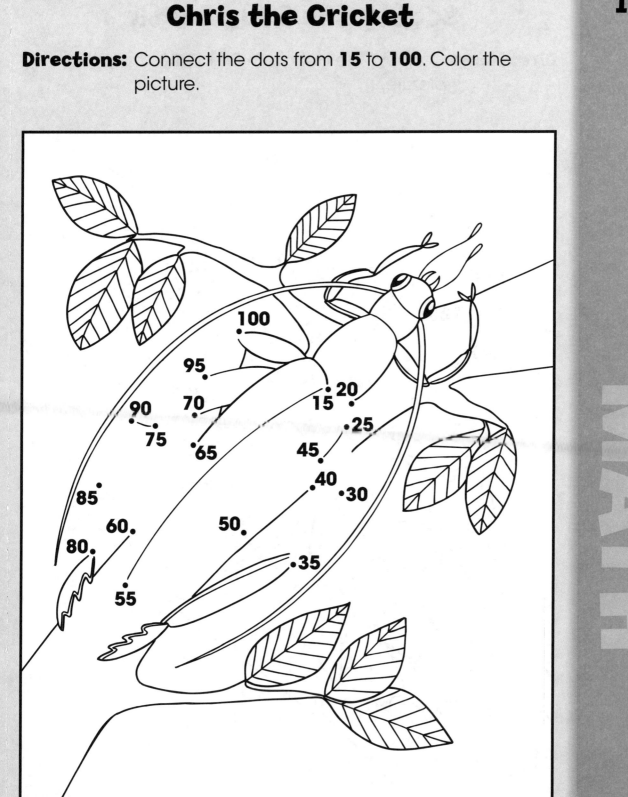

MATH

One Step Further

Crickets chirp. With a friend, use different kinds of chirps to make up a secret code.

Scotty the Stag Beetle

Directions: Connect the dots from **50** to **200**. Color the picture.

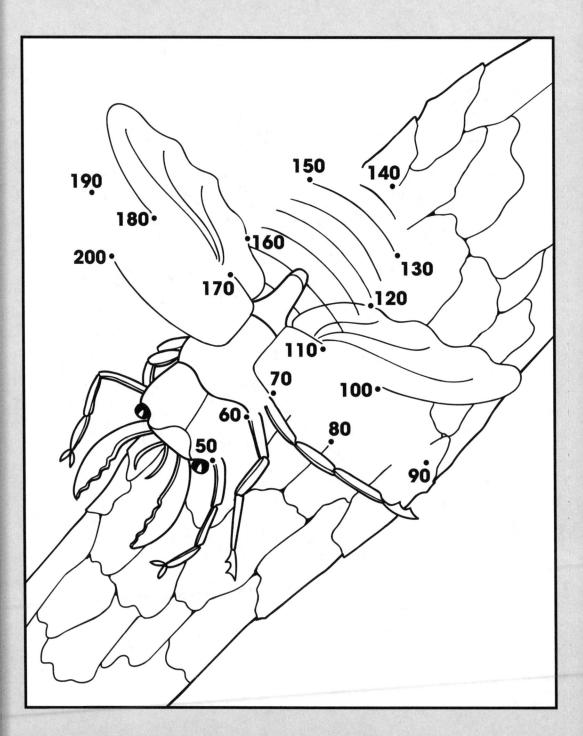

One Step Further

In **beetle**, the long **e** sound is spelled **ee**.
Make a list of more words with **ee**.

Barry the Beetle

Directions: Connect the dots from **10** to **200**. Color the picture.

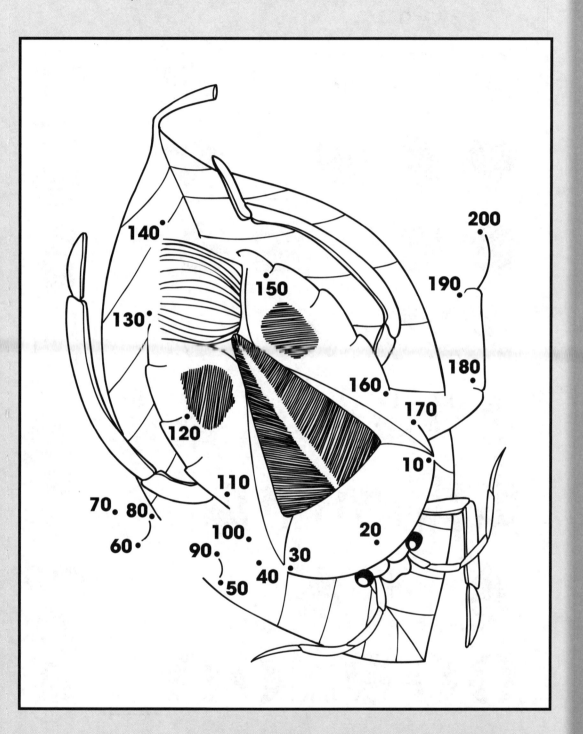

One Step Further
Count to 100 by 1s, 2s, 5s, and 10s. Jump or clap each time you count.

Sizable Patterns

Directions: Look at each pattern. Connect the missing picture to each pattern. Not all pictures will be used.

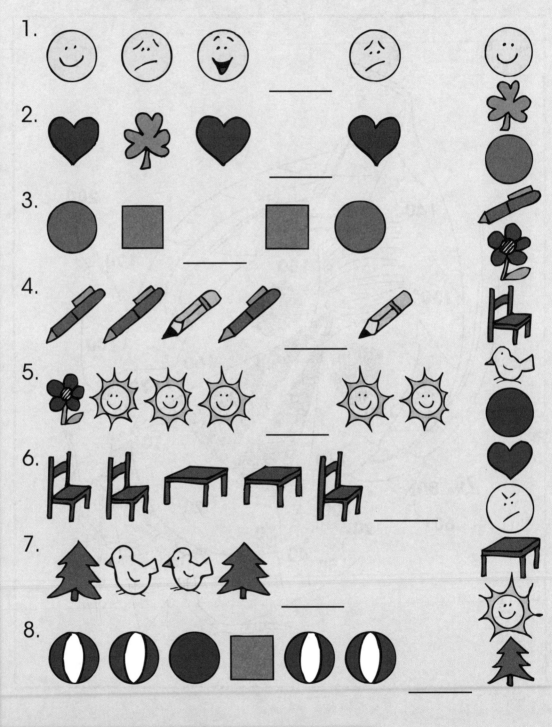

1.
2.
3.
4.
5.
6.
7.
8.

MATH

One Step Further
Design a T-shirt that includes a pattern of your very own.

Square, Square, Circle

Directions: Look at the patterns. Draw in each missing shape.

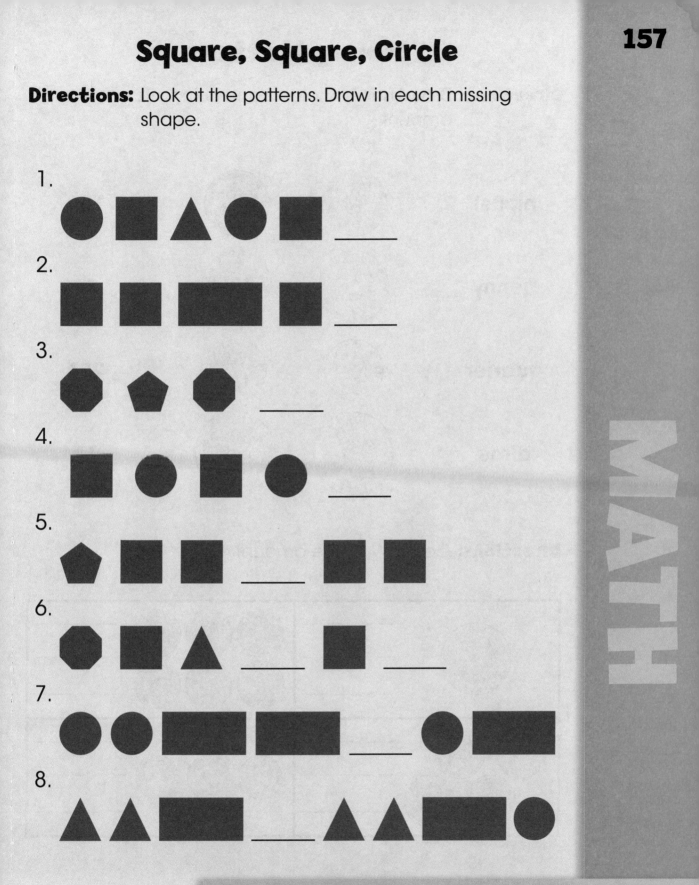

1. ⬤ ◼ ▲ ⬤ ◼ ____

2. ◼ ◼ ▬ ◼ ____

3. ⯃ ⬠ ⯃ ____

4. ◼ ⬤ ◼ ⬤ ____

5. ⬠ ◼ ◼ ____ ◼ ◼

6. ⯃ ◼ ▲ ____ ◼ ____

7. ⬤ ⬤ ▬ ▬ ____ ⬤ ▬

8. ▲ ▲ ▬ ____ ▲ ▲ ▬ ⬤

One Step Further

Look around your bedroom for patterns. You might be surprised at what you find!

MATH

Money Matters

Directions: Draw lines to match each coin to its name and amount.

nickel   10¢

penny   5¢

quarter   25¢

dime   1¢

Directions: Count. Write the amount.

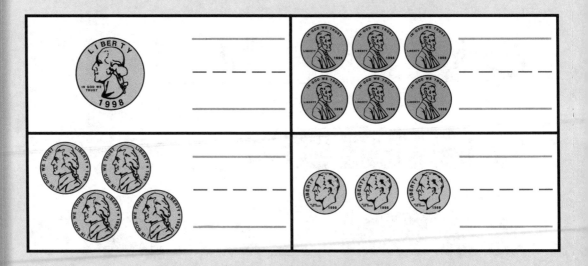

One Step Further

Look around your home for all the loose change you can find. Count it.

Toy Store Fun

| 5¢ | 10¢ | 15¢ | 20¢ | 25¢ | 30¢ | 35¢ | 40¢ | 45¢ |

Directions: Skip count by fives to count these nickels. Write the amount. Circle the toy with the matching price.

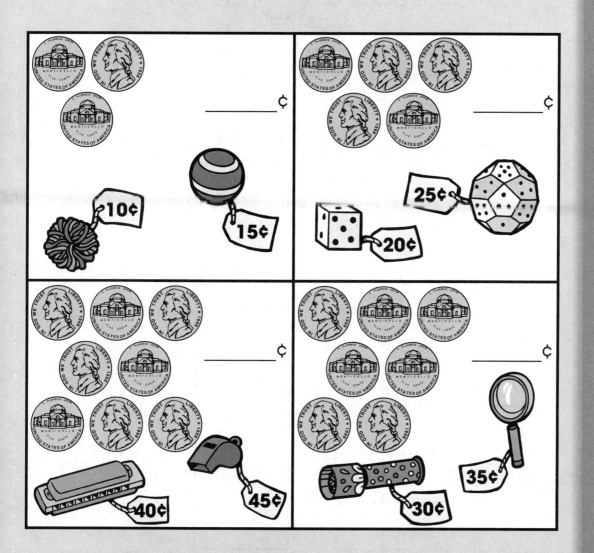

MATH

One Step Further

Is there something you want to buy? Start saving your money in a piggy bank!

First Grade Essentials

Prime Time

Directions: Read about Ed's day. Write the times in the puzzle.

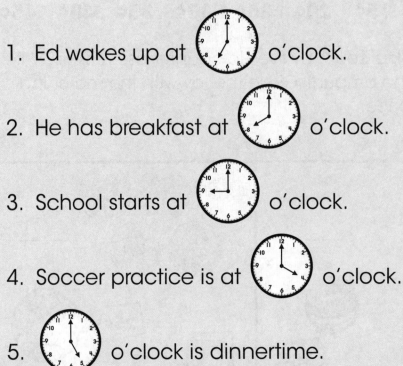

1. Ed wakes up at   o'clock.

2. He has breakfast at   o'clock.

3. School starts at   o'clock.

4. Soccer practice is at   o'clock.

5.   o'clock is dinnertime.

1.		:		
2.		:		
3.		:		
4.		:		
5.		:		

5:00

9:00

7:00

8:00

4:00

One Step Further

Do you do each of these things earlier than, later than, or at the same time as Ed?

A Long Day

Directions: Read about Ty's day. Write the times in the puzzle.

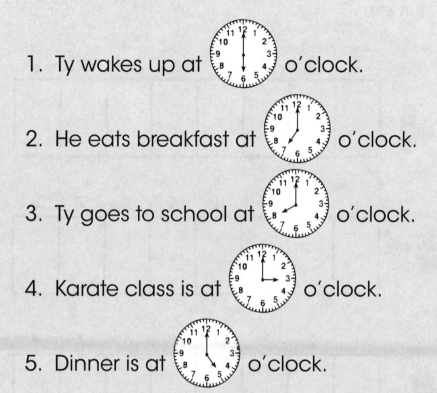

1. Ty wakes up at ⏰ o'clock.

2. He eats breakfast at ⏰ o'clock.

3. Ty goes to school at ⏰ o'clock.

4. Karate class is at ⏰ o'clock.

5. Dinner is at ⏰ o'clock.

MATH

1.		:		
2.		:		
3.		:		
4.		:		
5.		:		

| 5:00 |
| 6:00 |
| 3:00 |
| 8:00 |
| 7:00 |

One Step Further
Draw clocks that show what time you wake up, eat breakfast, and go to school.

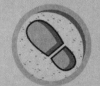

Take a Bite!

Directions: Count the apples in each row. Color the boxes to show how many apples have bites taken out of them.

Example:

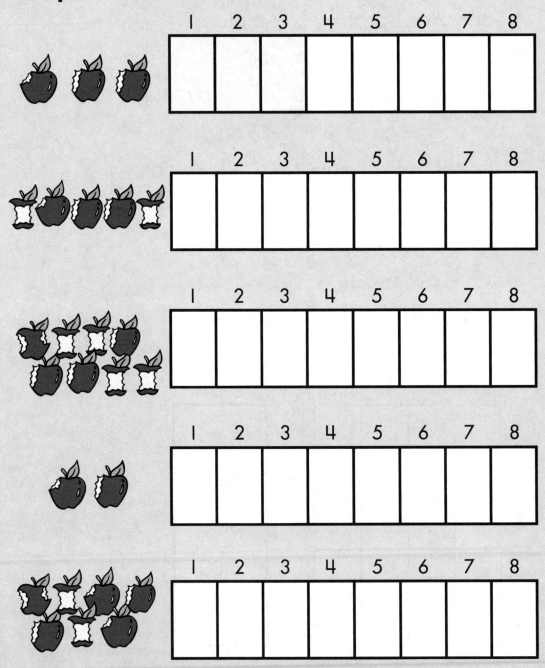

One Step Further

Eat an apple. How many bites does it take you to eat the whole apple?

Wormy Apples

Directions: Color the boxes to show how many worms are in each apple. Answer the questions at the bottom of the page.

	1	2	3	4	5	6
1						
2						
3						

How many worms are in apple 1? _____

How many worms are in apple 2? _____

How many worms are in apple 3? _____

How many more worms are in apple 2 than apple 3? _____

How many fewer worms are in apple 1 than apple 2? _____

One Step Further
Give an apple to your favorite teacher.
Tell him or her what you like about school.

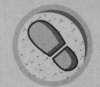

Graphing

Directions: Complete the graph below. Use the number of each animal you counted to fill in the rows with the missing pictures of turtles and dogs. The giraffes and sheep have been filled in for you.

	Column 1	Column 2	Column 3	Column 4	Column 5
🦒	🦒	🦒	🦒		
🐑	🐑	🐑			
🐢					
🐕					

Which animal cracker is there the most of? _____

Which animal cracker is there the fewest of? _____

_____

Three kinds of crackers have the same number. How many

are there? _____

One Step Further
Open a box of animal crackers.
Make a graph of the animals in the box.

Fantastic First Graders

Directions: Complete the table using the information shown. Then, answer the questions.

Class	Boys	Girls	Total
A		17	28
B	12	15	
C	9		23
Total			

1. Which class has the most students? _____

2. Which class has the fewest students? _____

3. How many more girls than boys are in the first grade? _____

4. Which class has the most boys? _____

5. Which class has the fewest girls? _____

6. How many students are in first grade? _____

7. How many more students are in class A than class C? _____

One Step Further
Make a graph of the boys and girls in your class at school.

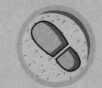

First Grade Essentials

Catfishing

I go fishing every Saturday!

This picture graph shows how many fish Cat caught.

First Saturday	🐟	🐟	🐟			
Second Saturday	🐟	🐟	🐟	🐟	🐟	🐟
Third Saturday	🐟	🐟	🐟	🐟		

Directions: Look at the graph and answer the questions below.

1. How many fish did Cat catch on the first Saturday? _____

2. How many more fish did he catch the next Saturday? _____

3. On which Saturday did Cat catch the most fish? _____

4. On which Saturday did Cat catch the fewest fish? _____

5. How many fish did Cat catch altogether? _____

One Step Further
What do you do every Saturday?
What do you do every Monday?

Food Fun

Directions: The table below tells what each animal brought to the picnic. Write the missing numbers.

Animal	Vegetables	Fruits	Total
Skunk	8	6	14
Raccoon	9		17
Squirrel		8	15
Rabbit	6		13
Owl	7		16
Deer		9	18

Directions: Write the name of the animal that answers each question.

1. Who brought the same number of vegetables as fruits? _____

2. Who brought two more fruits than vegetables? _____

3. Who brought two more vegetables than fruits? _____

4. Which two animals brought one more fruit than vegetable?

_____ and _____

5. Which two animals brought the most vegetables?

_____ and _____

6. Which two animals brought the most fruits?

_____ and _____

One Step Further

What fruits and vegetables would you bring to a picnic?

Honey Bear's Bakery

Directions: Color a space in the graph to show how many of each treat are in the bakery.

Number of Bakery Treats

12						
11						
10						
9						
8						
7						
6						
5						
4						
3						
2						
1						

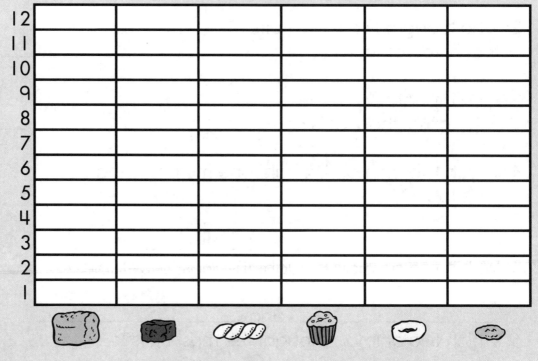

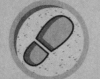

One Step Further

Name your favorite bakery treat. Which of these treats would you like to buy?

Amy's Things

Directions: Count the toys on Amy's shelf. Complete the table. Then, answer the questions.

Toy	How Many?

1. How many books and pigs are there altogether? _____

2. How many more teddy bears are there than cars? _____

3. Are there more dolls or animals? _____

4. Amy has four more _____

   than _____ .

5. Are there enough cars for each doll? _____

MATH

One Step Further

How many kinds of toys are on your toy shelf?
What toy do you have the most of?

Inch

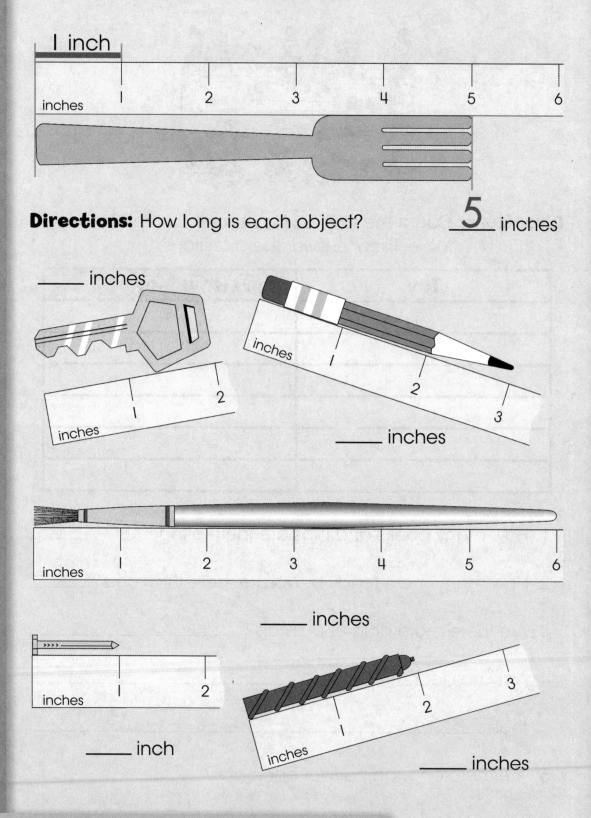

| 1 inch |

Directions: How long is each object?

_____ **5** inches

_____ inches

_____ inches

_____ inches

_____ inches

_____ inch

_____ inches

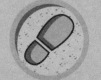

One Step Further

Find something in your home that is only one inch long.

Centimeter

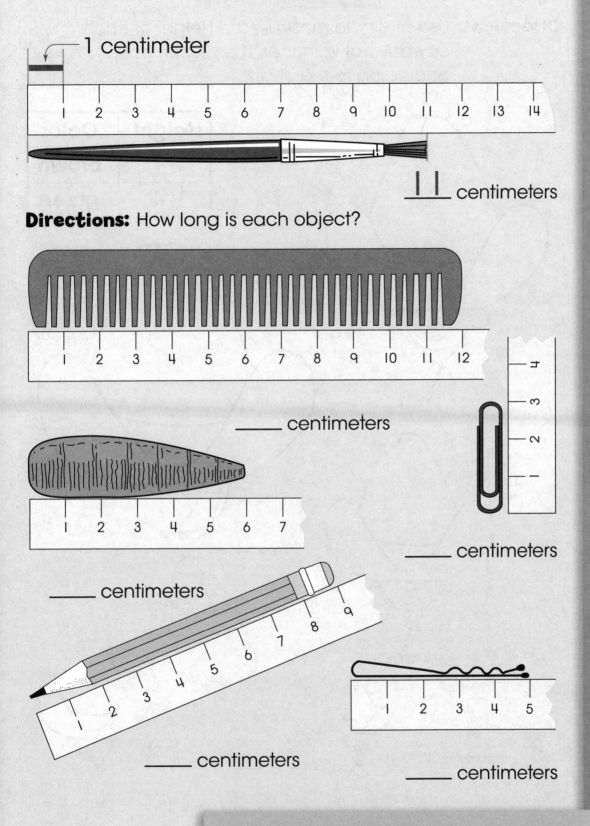

1 centimeter

1 2 3 4 5 6 7 8 9 10 11 12 13 14

_____ centimeters

Directions: How long is each object?

_____ centimeters

_____ centimeters

_____ centimeters

_____ centimeters

_____ centimeters

MATH

One Step Further
Go back to the object you found that was one inch long. How many centimeters is it?

Taking the Measurement

Directions: Use a ruler to measure the height of each cowboy hat in inches. Then, color each hat according to the chart.

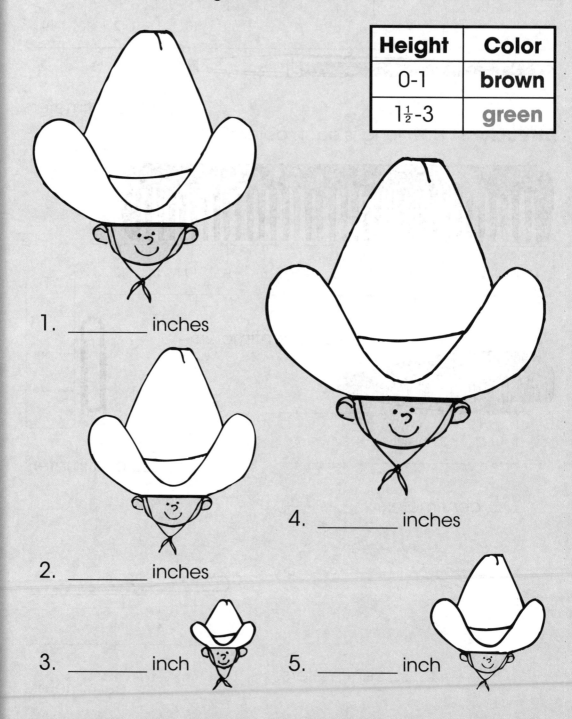

Height	Color
0-1	**brown**
$1\frac{1}{2}$-3	**green**

1. _____ inches

2. _____ inches

3. _____ inch

4. _____ inches

5. _____ inch

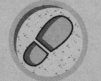

One Step Further

Find a tall, nonbreakable object. How long can you balance it on your head?

Flowers That "Measure" Up

Directions: Use a centimeter ruler to measure how tall each flower is. Measure each flower from the bottom of the stem to the top of the flower. Write the answer on the blank by the flower.

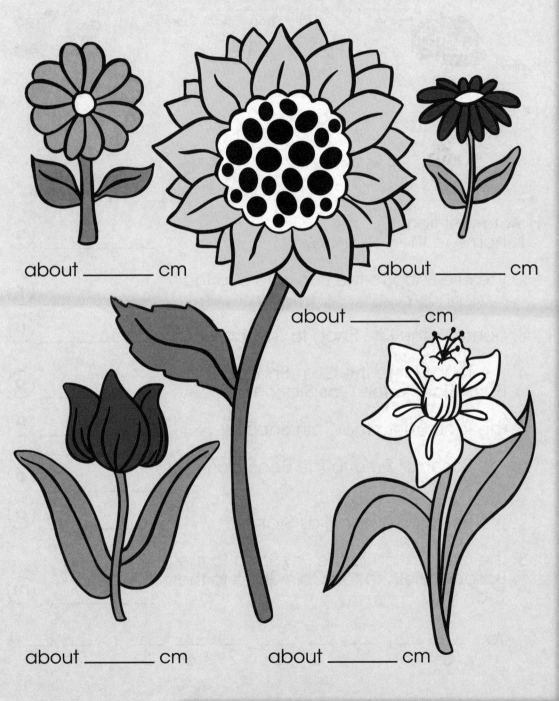

about _____ cm

about _____ cm

about _____ cm

about _____ cm

about _____ cm

MATH

One Step Further

Find a flower in your neighborhood. Measure it to the nearest centimeter.

First Grade Essentials

How Far Is It?

Directions: Use a ruler to measure each distance on the map in inches. Then, use the letters on the circles and your answers to solve the message at the bottom of the page.

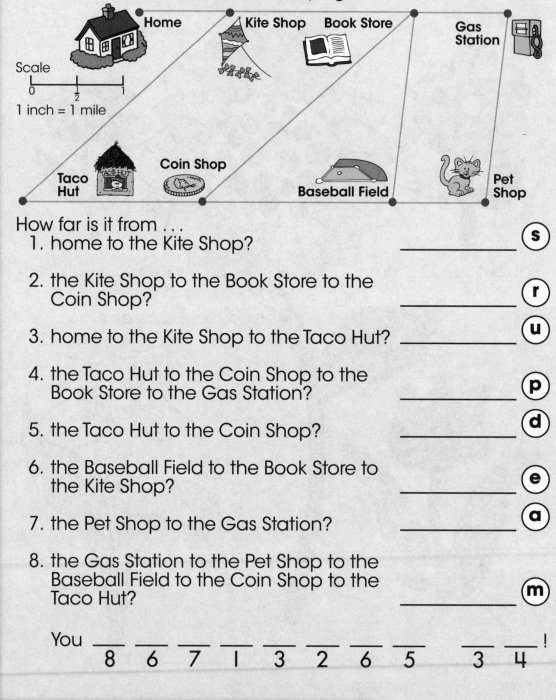

How far is it from . . .

1. home to the Kite Shop? _____ (s)

2. the Kite Shop to the Book Store to the Coin Shop? _____ (r)

3. home to the Kite Shop to the Taco Hut? _____ (u)

4. the Taco Hut to the Coin Shop to the Book Store to the Gas Station? _____ (p)

5. the Taco Hut to the Coin Shop? _____ (d)

6. the Baseball Field to the Book Store to the Kite Shop? _____ (e)

7. the Pet Shop to the Gas Station? _____ (a)

8. the Gas Station to the Pet Shop to the Baseball Field to the Coin Shop to the Taco Hut? _____ (m)

You ___ ___ ___ ___ ___ ___ ___ ___   ___ ___!
      8   6   7   1   3   2   6   5   3   4

One Step Further

How many miles is it from your home to your school? Ask an adult to help you find out.

Whole and Half

A **fraction** is a number that names part of a whole, such as $\frac{1}{4}$ or $\frac{1}{2}$.

Directions: Color half of each object.

Example:

Whole apple

Half an apple

$$\frac{1}{2}$$

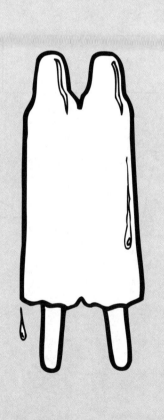

One Step Further
Which would you rather have: A whole candy bar or half a candy bar?

Thirds

Directions: Circle the objects that have three equal parts.

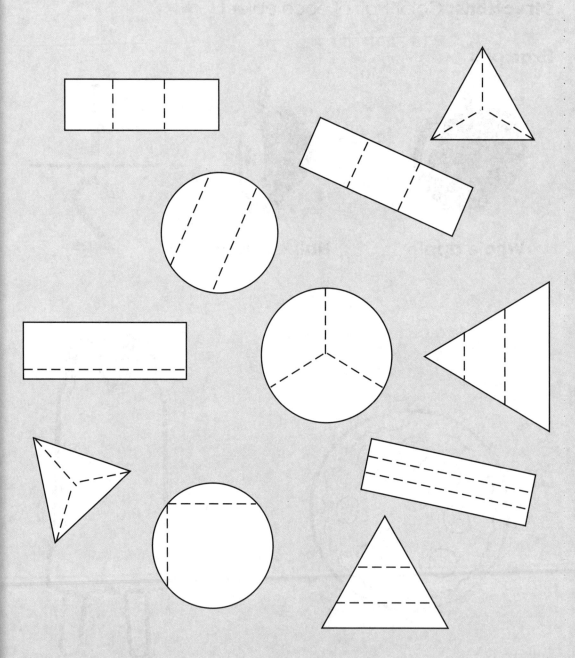

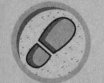

One Step Further

What's for dinner tonight?
Divide your food into three equal parts.

Fourths

Directions: Circle the objects that have four equal parts.

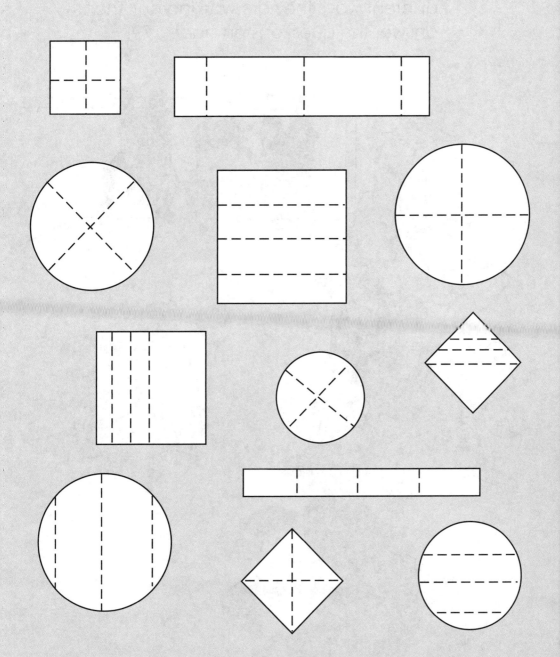

MATH

One Step Further
Ask an adult to cut an apple into four equal parts.

Fractions

The monsters are getting in shape.

Directions: Look below and on page 179 to see the different ways they are working out. Then, answer the questions on page 179.

One Step Further

What is your favorite way to get in shape?
Do you exercise with a friend?

Fractions

Directions: Answer the questions and fill in the blanks below. The first one is done for you.

How many monsters touch their toes?

___1___ out of 10 monsters, or $\dfrac{1}{10}$ of the monsters.

How many monsters hang upside down?

_____ out of 10 monsters, or $\dfrac{}{10}$ of the monsters.

How many of the monsters ride the bikes?

_____ out of 10 monsters, or $\dfrac{}{10}$ of the monsters.

How many of the monsters run on the treadmill?

_____ out of 10 monsters, or $\dfrac{}{10}$ of the monsters.

How many monsters lift weights?

_____ out of 10 monsters, or $\dfrac{}{10}$ of the monsters.

How many monsters do leg lifts?

_____ out of 10 monsters, or $\dfrac{}{10}$ of the monsters.

One Step Further
Touch your toes five times. Then, go outside and ride your bike with a friend.

Review

Directions: Count the equal parts. Then, write the fraction.

Example:

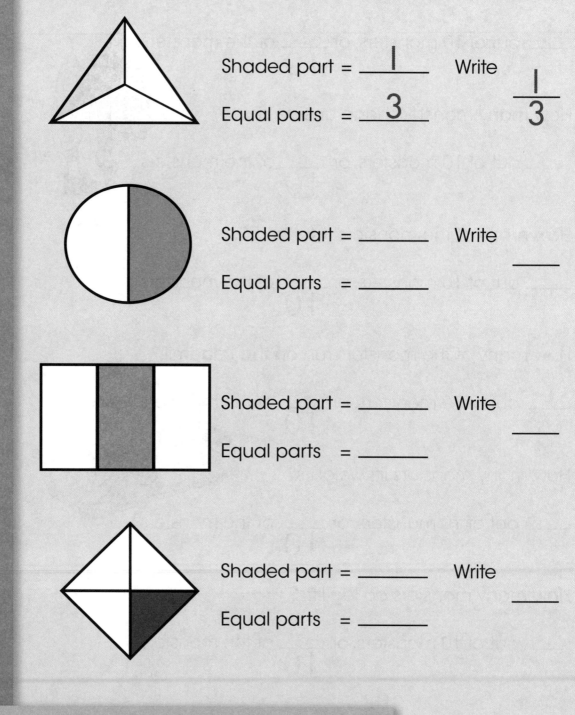

Shaded part = __1__   Write

Equal parts = __3__ $\frac{1}{3}$

Shaded part = _____   Write

Equal parts = _____   _____

Shaded part = _____   Write

Equal parts = _____   _____

Shaded part = _____   Write

Equal parts = _____   _____

One Step Further

Split a banana into two parts. Then, split the parts again. How many parts are there?

Games and Activities

Healthy Foods

Directions: Read the clues and use the words in the word box to complete the puzzle.

fruit

vegetable

bread

milk

meat

GAMES

Across

2. A bagel is a food from the ____ and cereal group.
3. A slice of cheese belongs to the ____ group.
4. An orange is a food from the ____ group.

Down

1. Broccoli is a food from the ____ group.
3. Chicken and eggs belong to the ____ group.

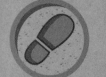

One Step Further

Say a color name. Can a friend think of healthy foods which have that color?

Things to Eat

Directions: Use the code to help you spell the food words.

1. ___ ___ ___ ___
   8   4   1   9

2. ___ ___ ___ ___ ___
  10 11 4 1 5

3. ___ ___ ___ ___
   3   7   9   6

4. ___ ___ ___ ___ ___ ___
   2   1   6   1   6   1

5. ___ ___ ___ ___ ___
   2   1   3   7   6

6. ___ ___ ___ ___ ___
  11 7 1 10 11

7. ___ ___ ___ ___
   3   1   5   4

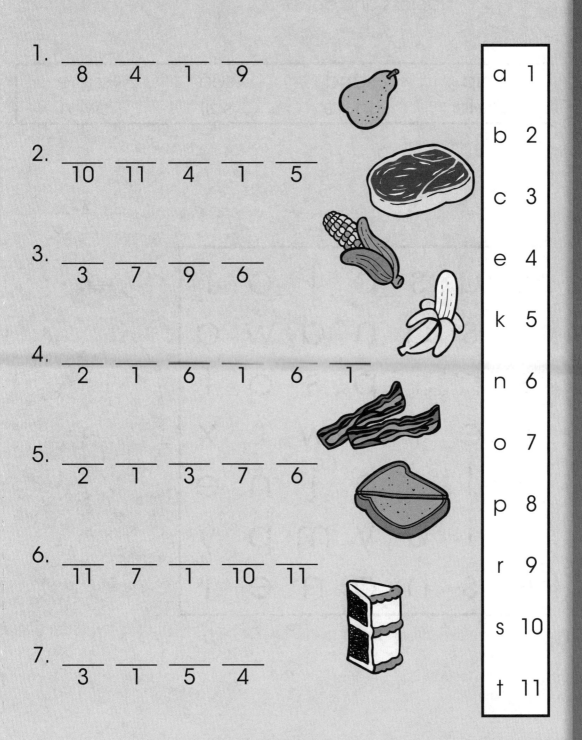

a	1
b	2
c	3
e	4
k	5
n	6
o	7
p	8
r	9
s	10
t	11

GAMES

One Step Further
Which of the foods on this page is your favorite? Which is your least favorite?

On the Shore

Directions: Circle the words in the puzzle. The words go across and down.

ship	sand	sun	shine
shells	shore	sail	swim

```
s  u  s  b  l  o  r
t  s  a  n  d  w  a
s  h  i  p  s  q  f
h  e  l  z  w  r  x
o  l  s  h  i  n  e
r  l  u  y  m  p  y
e  s  n  o  n  e  l
```

One Step Further

Draw a picture of a day at the shore. Include all of the objects on this page.

Fishy Friends

Directions: Help the striped fish swim through the coral and find its friend.

GAMES

One Step Further

Who is your best friend? Draw a picture of the two of you on the day you met.

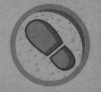

Dinosaurs

Directions: Read the clues and use the words in the word box to complete the puzzle.

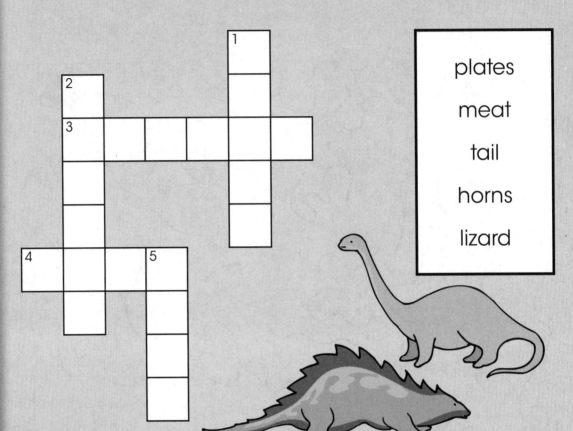

plates

meat

tail

horns

lizard

Across

3. The name **Brontosaurus** means "thunder ____."
4. A Tyrannosaurus was the largest ____-eating dinosaur.

Down

1. A Triceratops had three ____ and a massive shield.
2. A Stegosaurus had huge bony ____ along its back.
5. An Ankylosaurus had a heavy club at the end of its ____.

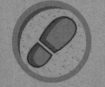

One Step Further

If you could be a dinosaur, which would you want to be? Why?

Draw a Dinosaur

Directions: These pictures are out of order. Number the steps from **1** to **6**.

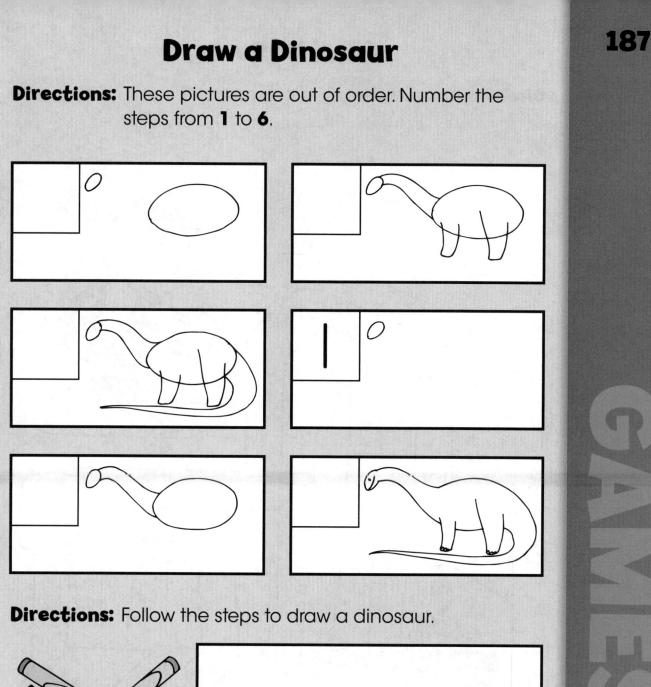

Directions: Follow the steps to draw a dinosaur.

One Step Further

What other animals can you draw using this method? See if you can teach a friend.

GAMES

Mail Delivery

Directions: Lead the pig to the mailbox.

One Step Further

What is the best thing you've ever gotten in the mail?

Mail Call

Directions: Unscramble the words that have to do with mail.

1. rettles __ __ __ __ __ __ __

2. cpageksa __ __ __ __ __ __ __ __

3. tpamss __ __ __ __ __ __

4. ilam rrcaire __ __ __ __ __ __ __ __ __ __ __

5. tsop oceiff __ __ __ __ __ __ __ __ __ __

6. axombli __ __ __ __ __ __ __

7. leeydivr __ __ __ __ __ __ __ __

8. dracs __ __ __ __ __

delivery	mail carrier	
letters	stamps	packages
mailbox	cards	post office

One Step Further

Write a friendly letter to a friend or family member. Ask an adult to help you mail it.

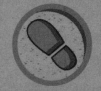

Park the Car

Directions: Drive the car to the garage.

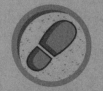

One Step Further
Create a map of the street you live on.
Include landmarks like trees and stop signs.

A Neighborhood

Directions: Read the clues and use the words in the word box to complete the puzzle.

house

street

school

store

sidewalk

park

GAMES

Across

1. The children go to _____.
4. Latasha and Ryan walked on the _____.
5. Mom and Dad went to the _____ to buy groceries.

Down

2. Tyana lives in the blue _____ on the corner.
3. The children play in the _____.
4. Cars drive up and down the _____.

One Step Further

On a large sheet of paper, draw a map of your street or neighborhood.

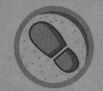

First Grade Essentials

Toy Time

Directions: Circle the words in the puzzle. The words go across and down.

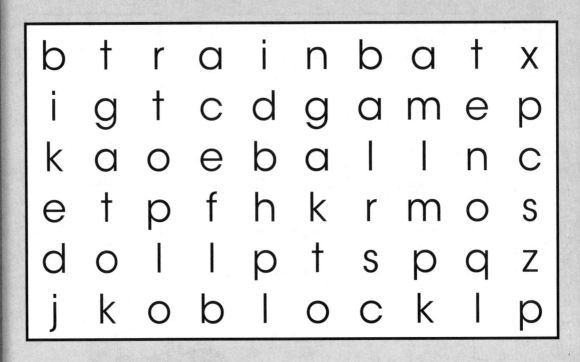

```
b t r a i n b a t x
i g t c d g a m e p
k a o e b a l l n c
e t p f h k r m o s
d o l l p t s p q z
j k o b l o c k l p
```

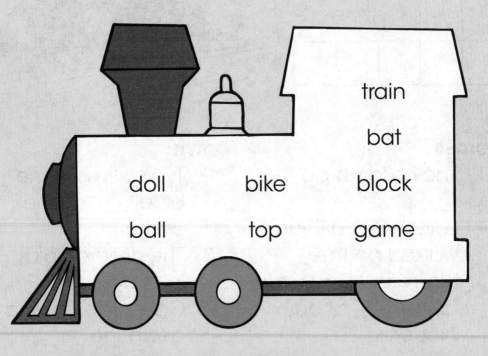

train
bat
doll   bike   block
ball   top   game

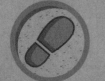

One Step Further

Gather up some of your old toys and donate them to someone in need.

First Grade Essentials

Time to Clean Up

Directions: Take the toys to the toy box.

One Step Further
Go through some old toys or books. You
might discover a fond memory!

Shining Bright

Directions: To find the mystery letter, color the spaces with the following letters **red**.

Q F V P G O M N U S

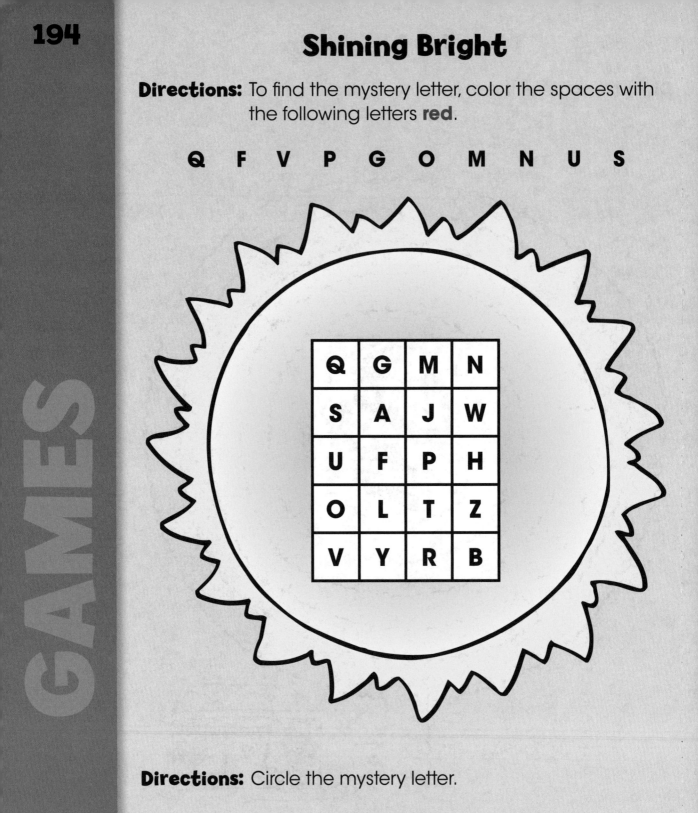

Q	G	M	N
S	A	J	W
U	F	P	H
O	L	T	Z
V	Y	R	B

Directions: Circle the mystery letter.

E   F   P

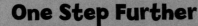

One Step Further
Name five objects that you could describe as shiny.

St Is for Star

Directions: Fill in the blanks with **s, sl, sm, sn,** or **st**. Circle the words in the puzzle. The words go across and down.

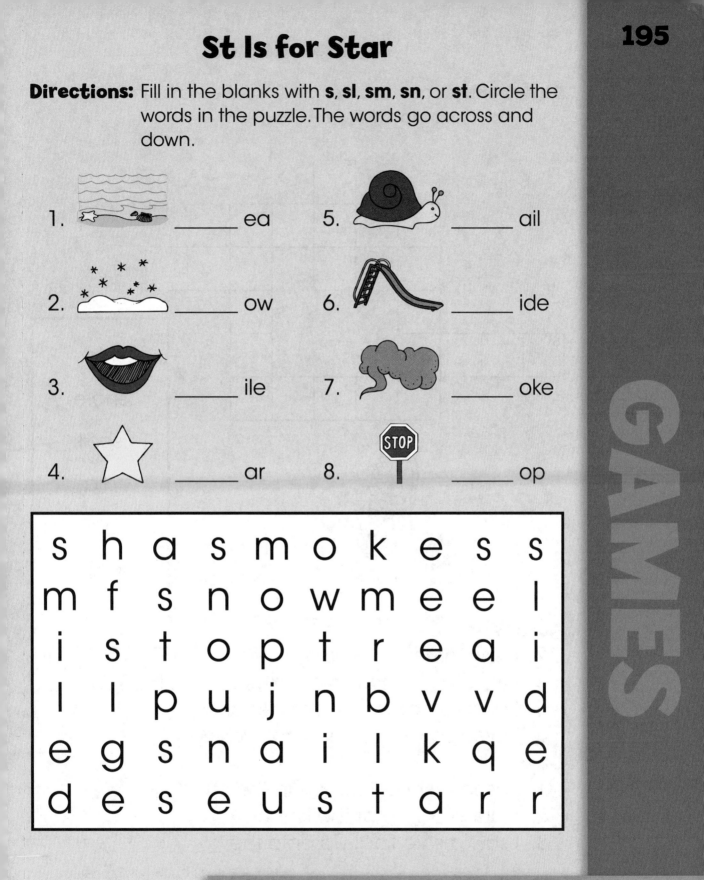

1. _____ ea

2. _____ ow

3. _____ ile

4. _____ ar

5. _____ ail

6. _____ ide

7. _____ oke

8. _____ op

s	h	a	s	m	o	k	e	s	s
m	f	s	n	o	w	m	e	e	l
i	s	t	o	p	t	r	e	a	i
l	l	p	u	j	n	b	v	v	d
e	g	s	n	a	i	l	k	q	e
d	e	s	e	u	s	t	a	r	r

One Step Further

List as many words you can think of with the consonant blends on this page.

GAMES

First Grade Essentials

At the Beach

Directions: Read the clues and use the words in the word box to complete the puzzle.

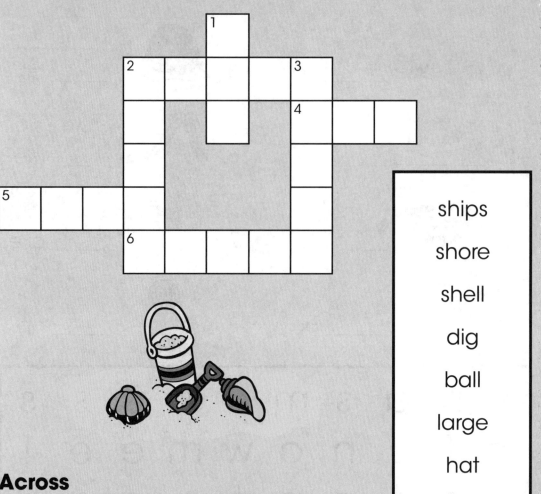

ships

shore

shell

dig

ball

large

hat

Across

2. I saw three ____ sail by.
4. I wore a ____ to protect myself from the sun.
5. I played catch with my beach ____.
6. I even saw a dolphin that was very ____.

Down

1. I used a shovel to ____ in the sand.
2. I found a ____ at the beach.
3. I saw a ship float up onto the ____.

One Step Further

Tell a story about a day at the beach. Make up characters for your story.

Underwater

Directions: Circle the words in the puzzle. The words go across and down.

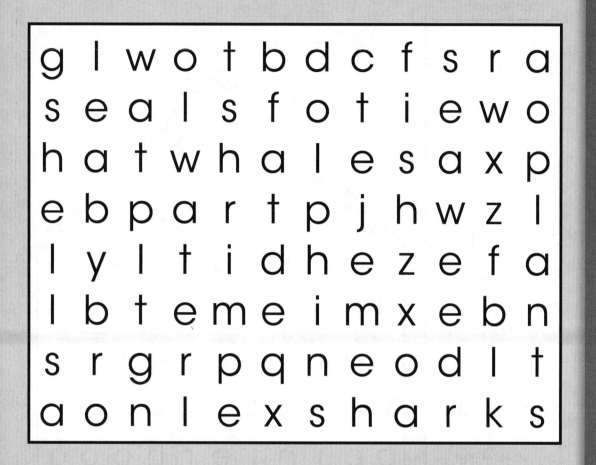

```
g l w o t b d c f s r a
s e a l s f o t i e w o
h a t w h a l e s a x p
e b p a r t p j h w z l
l y l t i d h e z e f a
l b t e m e i m x e b n
s r g r p q n e o d l t
a o n l e x s h a r k s
```

water	seals
sharks	fish
shrimp	plants
shells	whales
dolphins	seaweed

One Step Further

What is your favorite underwater creature?
Have you ever seen one in real life?

Breeds of Dogs

Directions: Circle the words in the puzzle. The words go across and down.

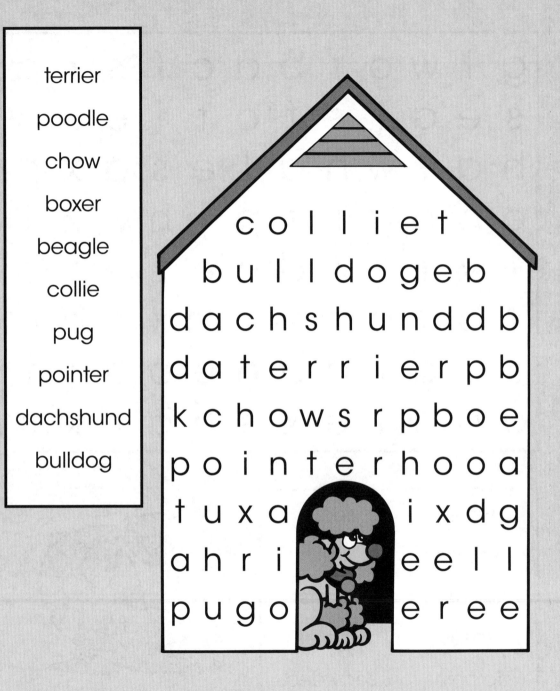

terrier

poodle

chow

boxer

beagle

collie

pug

pointer

dachshund

bulldog

```
c o l l i e t
b u l l d o g e b
d a c h s h u n d d b
d a t e r r i e r p b
k c h o w s r p b o e
p o i n t e r h o o a
t u x a      i x d g
a h r i      e e l l
p u g o      e r e e
```

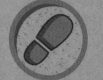

One Step Further

Some breeds of dogs are small and some
are big. Which do you prefer? Why?

Lost Collar

Directions: Help the puppy find its collar.

One Step Further
Design a fancy doghouse. What could you put inside?

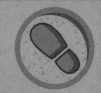

Crack the Code

Directions: Use the code to write the missing letters for each word.

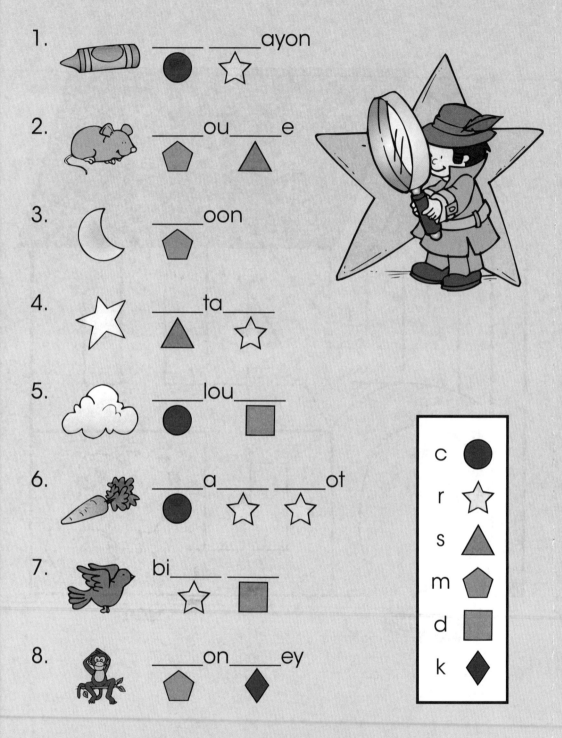

1. _____ _____ayon
   ● ☆

2. _____ou_____e
   ⬠ △

3. _____oon
   ⬠

4. _____ta_____
   △ ☆

5. _____lou_____
   ● ▢

6. _____a_____ _____ot
   ● ☆ ☆

7. bi_____ _____
   ☆ ▢

8. _____on_____ey
   ⬠ ◆

c	●
r	☆
s	△
m	⬠
d	▢
k	◆

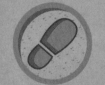

One Step Further
Create symbols for all letters of the alphabet.
Write a message using your symbols.

First Grade Essentials

Fix These Words

Directions: Unscramble the letters. Use the pictures to help you. Write the words on the lines.

g p i

r a t s

u n s

d e b

t h a

n f a

t e n s

u b s

One Step Further

Look outside and write five things you see.
Scramble their names and let a friend solve.

GAMES

Picture Clues

Directions: Letters, numbers, and pictures take the place of words in each sentence below. Write each sentence correctly.

R are		🥫 can		**U** you	
8 ate		👁 I		m 👁 my	

1. 👁 **8** an apple.

_____

- - - - - - - - - - - - - - - - - - - -

_____

2. **R U** happy?

_____

- - - - - - - - - - - - - - - - - - - -

_____

3. 🥫 **U** see me?

_____

- - - - - - - - - - - - - - - - - - - -

_____

4. 👁 🥫 see **U**.

_____

- - - - - - - - - - - - - - - - - - - -

_____

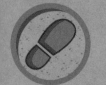

One Step Further

Write a message to a friend using the code.
Create other symbols if you want to.

Secret Word

Directions: Use the clues to help you fill in the puzzles.

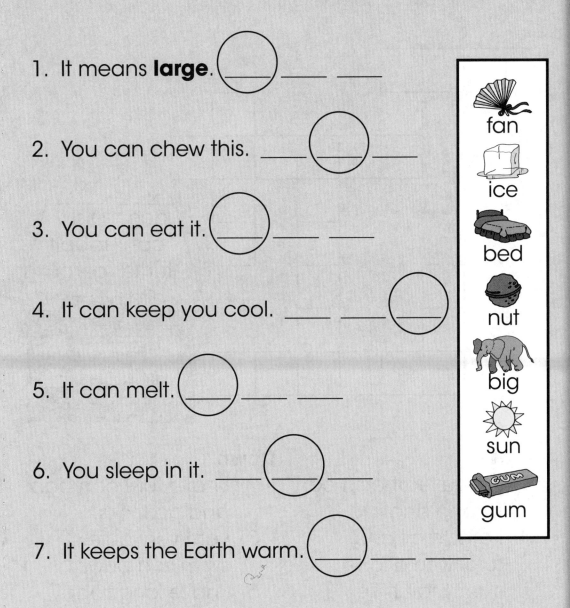

1. It means **large**. ◯__ __ __

2. You can chew this. __ ◯__ __

3. You can eat it. ◯__ __ __

4. It can keep you cool. __ __ ◯__

5. It can melt. ◯__ __ __

6. You sleep in it. __ ◯__ __

7. It keeps the Earth warm. ◯__ __ __

fan
ice
bed
nut
big
sun
gum

Directions: Find the secret word by writing the circled letters in order.

__ __ __ __ __ __ __

One Step Further
Create a secret code like the one above. See if a friend can solve your secret word.

At the Pet Shop

Directions: Read the clues and use the words in the word box to complete the puzzle.

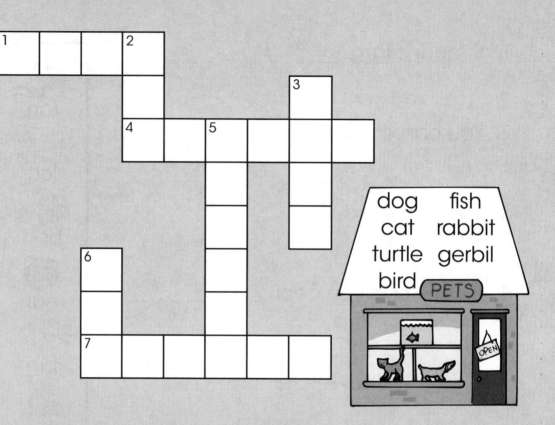

GAMES

Across

1. I have feathers. I can fly and sing.
4. I am small and furry with a long skinny tail. I like running around on a wheel.
7. I have a hard shell. I walk very slowly.

Down

2. I have fur. I can bark and do tricks.
3. I am very quiet. I swim in a bowl.
5. I have long floppy ears and a fluffy round tail. I like eating carrots.
6. I am furry. When you pet me I purr.

One Step Further

Write another riddle about a pet. See if a friend can guess the correct answer.

Pet Time

Directions: Look in the bone for the things you might need for a new pet. Write the words in the puzzle.

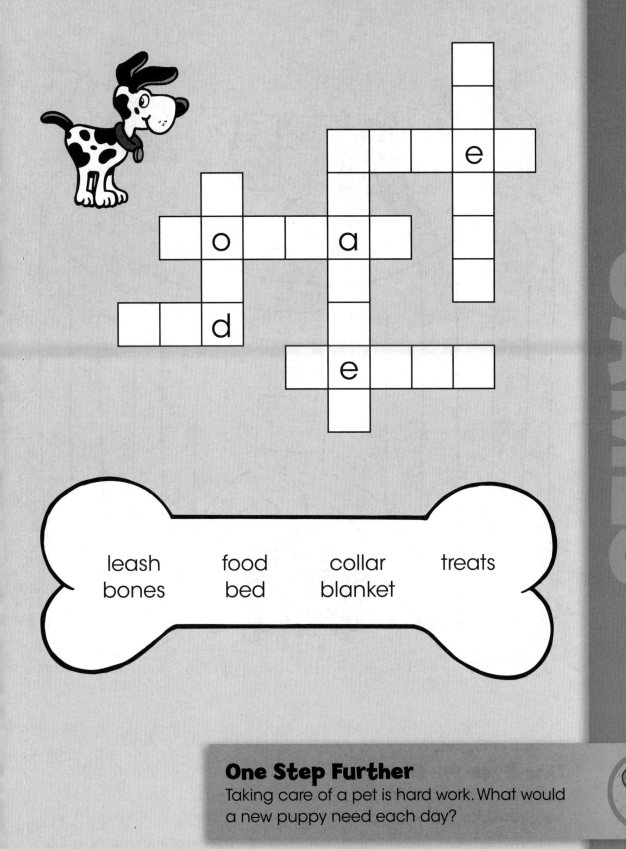

leash   food   collar   treats
bones   bed   blanket

GAMES

One Step Further
Taking care of a pet is hard work. What would a new puppy need each day?

All Dry

Directions: The clothes are dry. Help put them in the basket.

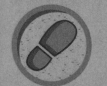

One Step Further

Randomly choose a shirt and pair of pants from your closet. Enjoy your fun new outfit!

Around the House

Directions: Read the clues and use the words in the word box to complete the puzzle.

| locks | sink | bedroom | windows |
| porch | doors | kitchen | living room |

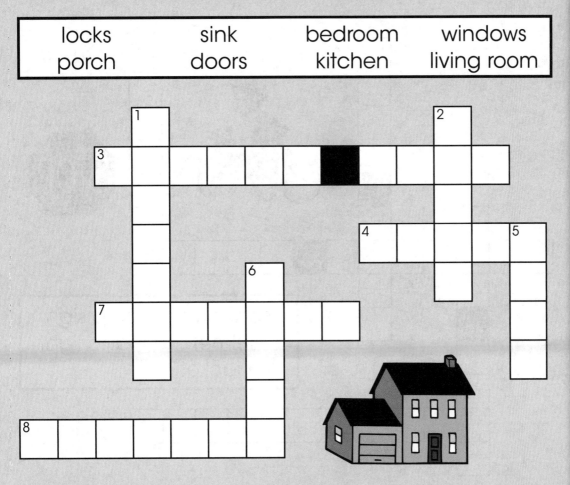

GAMES

Across

3. It is a room for entertaining.
4. These keep people out.
7. It is a room for sleeping.
8. You see through these.

Down

1. It is a place to cook.
2. It is outside of the house.
5. You wash your hands here.
6. You can enter through these.

One Step Further

Use four words to describe your bedroom. Then, use different words for your kitchen.

Safety

Directions: Read the clues and use the words in the word box to complete the puzzle.

seat belt   stop sign
helmet   traffic light
life jacket

GAMES

Across
4. I tell cars when to stop and go.
5. I help you keep afloat when you are in the water.

Down
1. I am red with white letters. I sit on a post.
2. You wear me on your head when you ride a bike.
3. You wear me when you ride in a car.

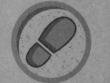

One Step Further
Invent something that helps keep you safe on the playground. Draw it.

Being a Friend

Directions: Read the clues and use the words in the word box to complete the puzzle.

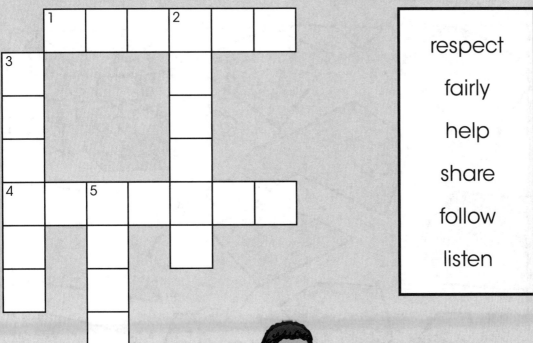

respect

fairly

help

share

follow

listen

Across

1. ____ the rules.
4. ____ others' feelings.
6. ____ others.

Down

2. ____ when others are talking.
3. Treat others ____.
5. ____ with others.

One Step Further

What do you think is most important for being a good friend?

A Cold Walk

Directions: Help the penguin find its way to the igloo.

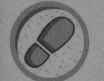

One Step Further

Igloo begins and ends with a vowel. Name other words that follow this pattern.

Scott's Sled

Directions: Show Scott the trail to his sled.

One Step Further
What is your favorite winter activity? Do you prefer being indoors or outdoors?

Field Goal

Directions: Kick the football through the goalposts.

One Step Further
Choreograph your own touchdown dance.
Perform it until you have it memorized.

GAMES

Figure Them Out!

Directions: Unscramble each word. Be sure that it matches the meaning.

teacher	ice cream	apple
mouse	jogger	tennis

1. Someone who runs is called a

   rjggeo ___ ___ ___ ___ ___ ___.

2. A game that uses a racket and a small ball is

   stinne ___ ___ ___ ___ ___ ___.

3. Something cold to eat on a hot day is

   cie ramec ___ ___ ___ ___ ___ ___ ___ ___.

4. Someone who teaches children is a

   erhteac ___ ___ ___ ___ ___ ___ ___.

5. A tasty fruit that grows on a tree is called an

   leppa ___ ___ ___ ___ ___.

6. A furry little animal that squeaks is a

   somue ___ ___ ___ ___ ___.

GAMES

One Step Further

Scramble five more words for a friend. Give him or her clues to help find the answer.

In a City

Directions: Read the clues and use the words in the word box to complete the puzzle.

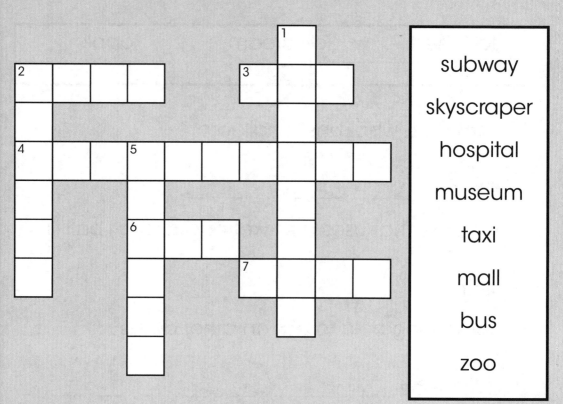

Word Box:
- subway
- skyscraper
- hospital
- museum
- taxi
- mall
- bus
- zoo

Across

2. This is a place with many stores in one building.
3. This is a place where many animals live.
4. This is a very tall building.
6. Many people ride in this on city streets.
7. People whistle, yell, or wave to get a ride in this thing.

Down

1. This is a place where people go when they are sick.
2. People visit this place to see very old things.
5. This train goes underground and people ride it.

One Step Further

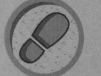

What large city is near your home? Find it on a map.

Around the World

Directions: Read the clues and use the words in the word box to complete the puzzle.

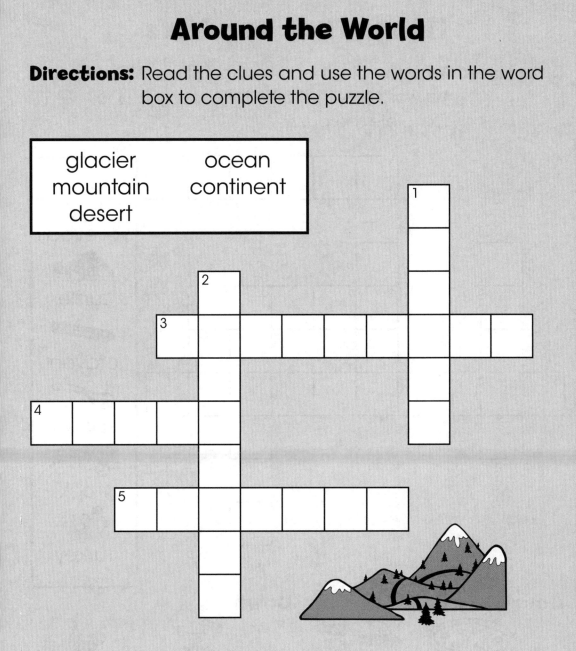

glacier ocean
mountain continent
desert

Across
3. A very large area of land
4. A very large body of water
5. A river of ice that seems to stand still

Down
1. A hot, dry area
2. A very high hill

One Step Further
There are seven continents and four oceans. How many can you name?

Things That Are Alike

Directions: Read the clues and find the other things from the word box that go with each group to complete the puzzle.

GAMES

volleyball

turtle

crayon

spoon

truck

turkey

Across

1. pizza   sandwich

3. car   motorcycle

5. basketball   baseball

Down

1. dog   cat

2. knife   fork

4. pencil   marker

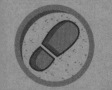

One Step Further

Tell a friend two things that go together. Can your friend think of a third?

Musical Instruments

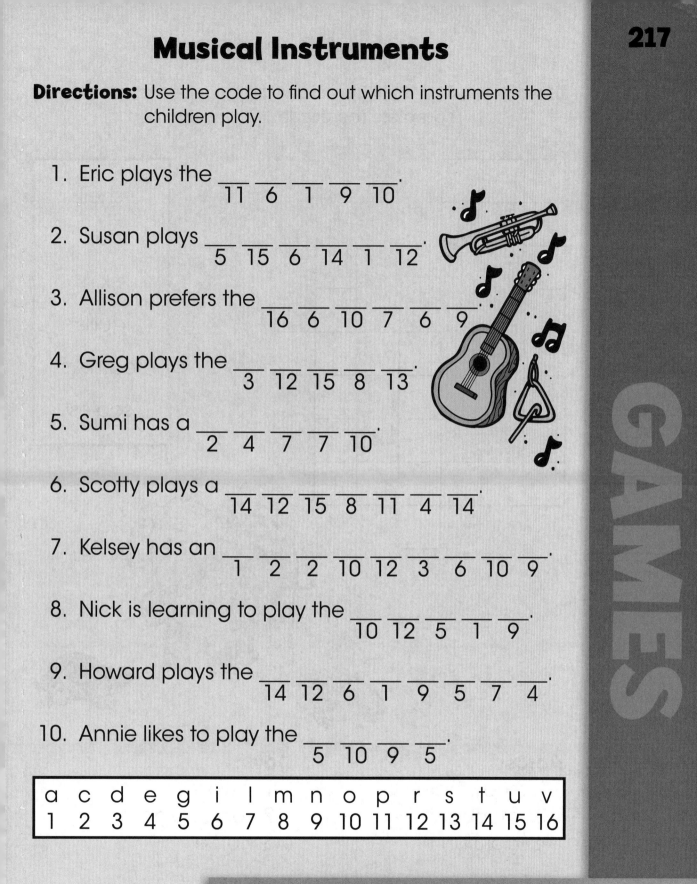

Directions: Use the code to find out which instruments the children play.

1. Eric plays the ___ ___ ___ ___ ___ .
   11 6 1 9 10

2. Susan plays ___ ___ ___ ___ ___ ___ .
   5 15 6 14 1 12

3. Allison prefers the ___ ___ ___ ___ ___ ___ .
   16 6 10 7 6 9

4. Greg plays the ___ ___ ___ ___ ___ .
   3 12 15 8 13

5. Sumi has a ___ ___ ___ ___ ___ .
   2 4 7 7 10

6. Scotty plays a ___ ___ ___ ___ ___ ___ ___ .
   14 12 15 8 11 4 14

7. Kelsey has an ___ ___ ___ ___ ___ ___ ___ ___ ___ .
   1 2 2 10 12 3 6 10 9

8. Nick is learning to play the ___ ___ ___ ___ ___ .
   10 12 5 1 9

9. Howard plays the ___ ___ ___ ___ ___ ___ ___ ___ .
   14 12 6 1 9 5 7 4

10. Annie likes to play the ___ ___ ___ ___ .
    5 10 9 5

a	c	d	e	g	i	l	m	n	o	p	r	s	t	u	v
1	2	3	4	5	6	7	8	9	10	11	12	13	14	15	16

One Step Further

Which musical instrument do you want to learn how to play? Why?

GAMES

Animal Coverings

Directions: Find the type of covering for each animal to complete the puzzle.

shell

fur

skin

quills

feathers

scales

Across
1. snow hare
3. elephant
4. goldfish

Down
1. swan
2. porcupine
3. turtle

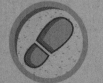

One Step Further
Which covering would you like to have for a day: quills, feathers, or scales? Why?

Work It Out

Directions: Look at the picture clues. Then, complete the puzzle using the words from the word box.

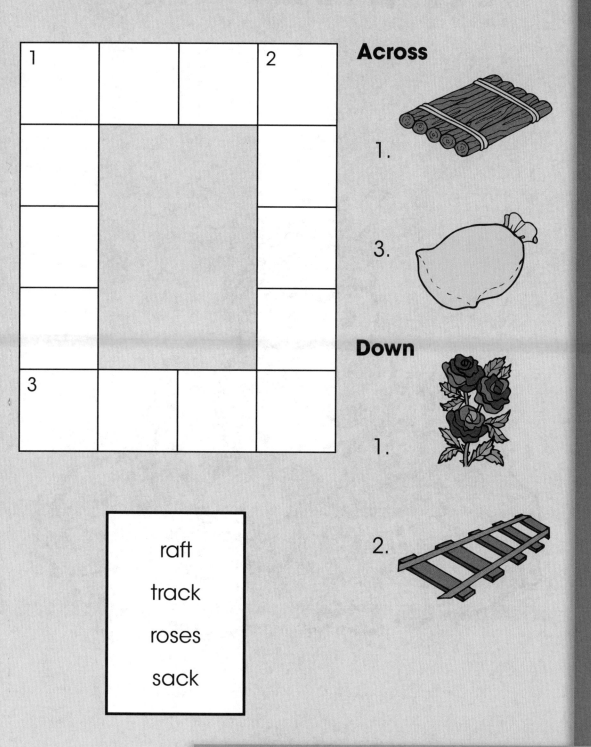

Across

1.

3.

Down

1.

2.

raft

track

roses

sack

First Grade Essentials

One Step Further
Draw a picture that includes all the objects on this page.

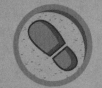

Answer Key

ANSWER KEY

6

ABC Order

Directions: Circle the first letter of each word. Then, put each pair of the words in **ABC** order.

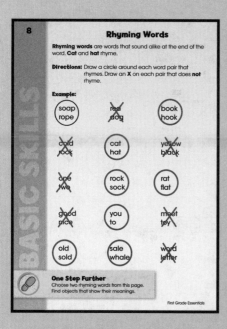

Car   Bird

bird
car

Moon   Two

moon
two

Nest   Fan

fan
nest

Card   Dog

card
dog

Pig   Bike

bike
pig

Sun   Pie

pie
sun

One Step Further
Write three words. Ask a friend to put them in ABC order.

First Grade Essentials

7

ABC Order

Directions: Look at the words in each box. Circle the word that comes first in **ABC** order.

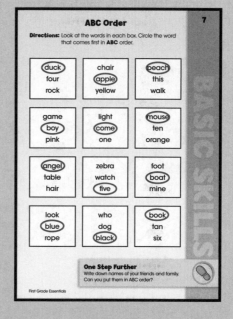

duck four rock	chair apple yellow	beach this walk
game boy pink	light come one	mouse ten orange
angel table hair	zebra watch five	foot boat mine
look blue rope	who dog black	book tan six

One Step Further
Write down names of your friends and family. Can you put them in ABC order?

First Grade Essentials

8

Rhyming Words

Rhyming words are words that sound alike at the end of the word. **Cat** and **hat** rhyme.

Directions: Draw a circle around each word pair that rhymes. Draw an **X** on each pair that does **not** rhyme.

Example:

soap rope   red dog   book hook

cold rock   cat hat   yellow black

one two   rock sock   rat flat

good nice   you to   meet toy

old sold   sale whale   word letter

One Step Further
Choose two rhyming words from this page. Find objects that show their meanings.

First Grade Essentials

9

Rhyming Words

Rhyming words are words that sound alike at the end of the word.

Directions: Draw a line to match the pictures that rhyme. Write two of your rhyming word pairs below.

Answers may include:

hat   cat
goat   coat

One Step Further
What word rhymes with your name? Make up a word if you have to!

First Grade Essentials

10

These Keep Me Warm

Directions: Color the things that keep you warm.

socks   apple   earmuffs   lunch box   cookie   coat   hat   umbrella   gloves   book

One Step Further
What do you do when you are cold? What clothes do you wear during the winter?

First Grade Essentials

11

Food Groups

Directions: Color the meats and eggs **brown**. Color the fruits and vegetables **green**. Color the breads **tan**. Color the dairy foods (milk and cheese)

fish   bread   apple   cheese
crackers   carrot   orange   eggs
steak   pear   milk   yogurt
ice cream   chicken   potato   pretzel

One Step Further
What is your favorite food from each of these food groups?

First Grade Essentials

First Grade Essentials

ANSWER KEY

BASIC SKILLS

BASIC SKILLS

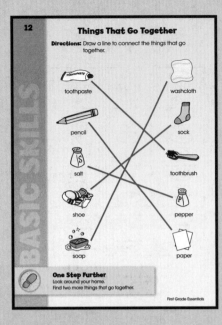

12

Things That Go Together

Directions: Draw a line to connect the things that go together.

- toothpaste
- pencil
- salt
- shoe
- soap
- washcloth
- sock
- toothbrush
- pepper
- paper

One Step Further
Look around your home.
Find two more things that go together.

First Grade Essentials

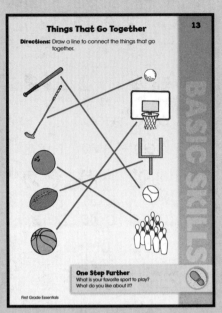

13

Things That Go Together

Directions: Draw a line to connect the things that go together.

One Step Further
What is your favorite sport to play?
What do you like about it?

First Grade Essentials

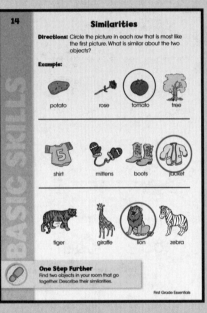

14

Similarities

Directions: Circle the picture in each row that is most like the first picture. What is similar about the two objects?

Example:

- potato
- rose
- tomato
- tree

- shirt
- mittens
- boots
- jacket

- tiger
- giraffe
- lion
- zebra

One Step Further
Find two objects in your room that go together. Describe their similarities.

First Grade Essentials

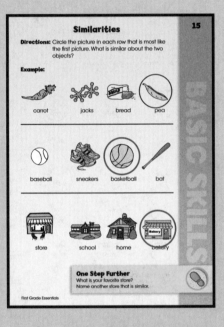

15

Similarities

Directions: Circle the picture in each row that is most like the first picture. What is similar about the two objects?

Example:

- carrot
- jacks
- bread
- pea

- baseball
- sneakers
- basketball
- bat

- store
- school
- home
- bakery

One Step Further
What is your favorite store?
Name another store that is similar.

First Grade Essentials

16

Things to Drink

Directions: Circle the pictures of things you can drink. Write the names of those things in the blanks.

- milk
- ice
- soup and crackers

- juice
- soda
- ice-cream bar

milk   soda

juice

One Step Further
Name something else you can drink.
What is your favorite thing to drink?

First Grade Essentials

17

Clowns and Balloons

Some words describe clowns. Some words describe balloons.

Directions: Read the words. Write the words in the correct columns.

| float | hat | air | pop |
| laughs | string | feet | nose |

laughs   float
hat   string
feet   air
nose   pop

One Step Further
How else could you describe a clown?
Tell a story about a clown to a friend.

First Grade Essentials

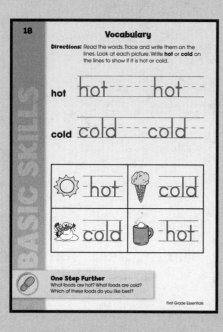

18

Vocabulary

Directions: Read the words. Trace and write them on the lines. Look at each picture. Write **hot** or **cold** on the lines to show if it is hot or cold.

hot   hot   hot

cold   cold   cold

hot   cold
cold   hot

One Step Further
What foods are hot? What foods are cold?
Which of these foods do you like best?

First Grade Essentials

19

Vocabulary

Directions: Read the words. Trace and write them on the lines. Look at each picture. Write **day** or **night** on the lines to show if they happen during the day or night.

day   day   day

night   night   night

night   day
night   day

One Step Further
What do you do during the day?
What do you do at night?

First Grade Essentials

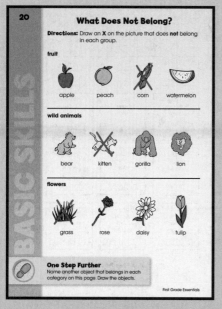

20

What Does Not Belong?

Directions: Draw an **X** on the picture that does **not** belong in each group.

fruit

apple   peach   corn   watermelon

wild animals

bear   kitten   gorilla   lion

flowers

grass   rose   daisy   tulip

One Step Further
Name another object that belongs in each category on this page. Draw the objects.

First Grade Essentials

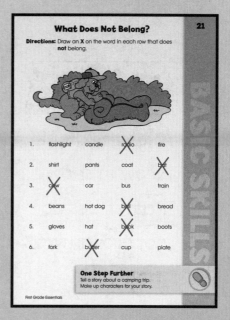

21

What Does Not Belong?

Directions: Draw an **X** on the word in each row that does **not** belong.

1. flashlight   candle   ~~radio~~   fire
2. shirt   pants   coat   ~~hat~~
3. ~~cow~~   car   bus   train
4. beans   hot dog   ~~ball~~   bread
5. gloves   hat   ~~book~~   boots
6. fork   ~~butter~~   cup   plate

One Step Further
Tell a story about a camping trip.
Make up characters for your story.

First Grade Essentials

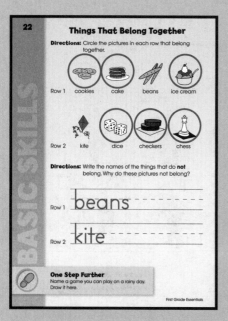

22

Things That Belong Together

Directions: Circle the pictures in each row that belong together.

Row 1   cookies   cake   beans   ice cream

Row 2   kite   dice   checkers   chess

Directions: Write the names of the things that do **not** belong. Why do these pictures not belong?

Row 1   beans

Row 2   kite

One Step Further
Name a game you can play on a rainy day.
Draw it here.

First Grade Essentials

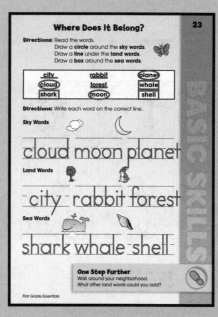

23

Where Does It Belong?

Directions: Read the words.
Draw a **circle** around the **sky words**.
Draw a **line** under the **land words**.
Draw a **box** around the **sea words**.

(city)	rabbit	[plane]
(cloud)	forest	[whale]
[shark]	(moon)	[shell]

Directions: Write each word on the correct line.

Sky Words

cloud moon planet

Land Words

city rabbit forest

Sea Words

shark whale shell

One Step Further
Walk around your neighborhood.
What other land words could you add?

First Grade Essentials

ANSWER KEY

24 — Menu Mix-Up

Directions: Circle names of **drinks** in red.
Circle names of **vegetables** in green.
Circle names of **desserts** in pink.

Directions: Write each food word on the correct line.

Drinks	Vegetables	Desserts
water	corn	cookie
juice	peas	pie
milk	carrot	cake

One Step Further
Pretend you own a restaurant.
What would be on your menu?

First Grade Essentials

25 — Word Sort

Directions: Circle words that name **colors** in red.
Circle words that name **shapes** in
Circle words that name **numbers** in green.

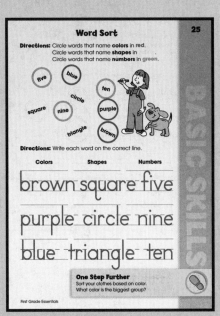

Directions: Write each word on the correct line.

Colors	Shapes	Numbers
brown	square	five
purple	circle	nine
blue	triangle	ten

One Step Further
Sort your clothes based on color.
What color is the biggest group?

First Grade Essentials

26 — What Does Not Belong?

Directions: Circle the two things that do not belong in the
picture. Write why they do not belong.

1. Flowers do not grow in snow.
2. Palm trees do not grow in snow.

One Step Further
Describe what is happening in the picture.
What winter activities do you enjoy?

First Grade Essentials

27 — Classification

Directions: The words in each box form a group. Choose
the word from the word box that describes each
group and write it on the line.

clothes	family	colors
flowers	fruits	animals
coins	toys	noises

rose buttercup tulip daisy **flowers**	crash bang ring pop **noises**	mother father sister brother **family**
puzzle wagon blocks doll **toys**	green purple blue red **colors**	grapes orange apple plum **fruits**
shirt socks dress coat **clothes**	dime penny nickel quarter **coins**	dog horse elephant moose **animals**

One Step Further
Look in your closet or drawer. What other
words could be classified as clothes?

First Grade Essentials

28 — Raking Leaves

Directions: Write a number in each box to show the order
of the story.

One Step Further
Go outside and find 10 leaves.
What color are the leaves?

First Grade Essentials

29 — Make a Snowman!

Directions: Write the number of the sentence that goes with
each picture in the box.

1. Roll a large snowball for the snowman's bottom.
2. Make another snowball and put it on top of the first.
3. Put the last snowball on top.
4. Dress the snowman.

One Step Further
Tell a story about building a snowman.
Have you ever built a snowman?

First Grade Essentials

30 — Color the Path

Directions: Color the path the girl should take to go home. Use the sentences to help you.

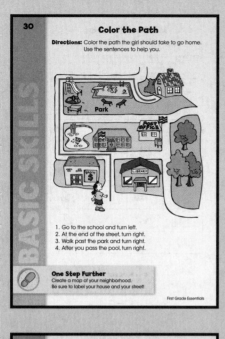

1. Go to the school and turn left.
2. At the end of the street, turn right.
3. Walk past the park and turn right.
4. After you pass the pool, turn right.

One Step Further
Create a map of your neighborhood. Be sure to label your house and your street!

First Grade Essentials

31 — Following Directions

Directions: Look at the pictures. Follow the directions in each box.

Draw a circle around the caterpillar. Draw a line under the stick.

Draw an **X** on the mother bird. Draw a triangle around the baby birds.

Draw a box around the rabbit.

Color the flowers. Count the bees. There are __2__ bees.

One Step Further
Draw a flower for a friend. Give your friend directions on how to color the flower.

First Grade Essentials

32 — Draw With Directions

Directions: Follow the directions to complete the picture.

1. Draw a smiling face on the sun.
2. Color the fish blue. Draw two more **blue** fish in the water.
3. Draw a **brown** bird under the cloud. Draw blue raindrops under the cloud.
4. Color the boat **red**. Color one sail **pink**. Color the other sail **green**.
5. Color the starfish **orange**. Draw two more **orange** starfish.

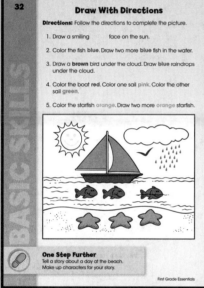

One Step Further
Tell a story about a day at the beach. Make up characters for your story.

First Grade Essentials

33 — Directions for Decorating

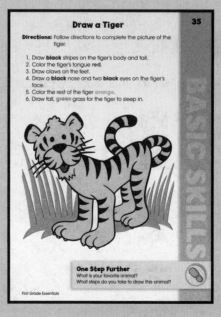

Directions: Follow the directions to decorate the bedroom.

Draw a **red** ▢ between the two 🔌 .

Draw a 🪑 under the window. Color it **green**.

Draw three big 🌸 on the wall. Color them **orange**.

Draw a picture of something you would like to have in your bedroom. Drawings will vary.

One Step Further
How is your room decorated? How would you like to decorate your room?

First Grade Essentials

34 — Following Directions

Follow the directions to make a paper sack puppet.

Directions: Find a small sack that fits your hand. Cut out teeth from colored paper. Glue them on the sack. Cut out ears. Glue them on the sack. Cut out eyes, a nose, and a tongue. Glue them all on.

Directions: Number the pictures **1, 2, 3,** and **4** to show the correct order.

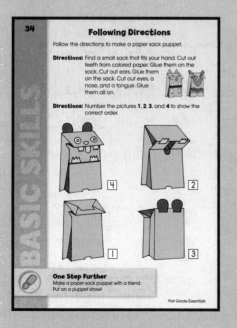

One Step Further
Make a paper sack puppet with a friend. Put on a puppet show!

First Grade Essentials

35 — Draw a Tiger

Directions: Follow directions to complete the picture of the tiger.

1. Draw **black** stripes on the tiger's body and tail.
2. Color the tiger's tongue **red**.
3. Draw claws on the feet.
4. Draw a **black** nose and two **black** eyes on the tiger's face.
5. Color the rest of the tiger **orange**.
6. Draw tall, **green** grass for the tiger to sleep in.

One Step Further
What is your favorite animal? What steps do you take to draw this animal?

First Grade Essentials

ANSWER KEY

36

Days of the Week

The days of the week begin with capital letters.

Directions: Write the days of the week in the spaces below. Put them in order. Be sure to start with capital letters.

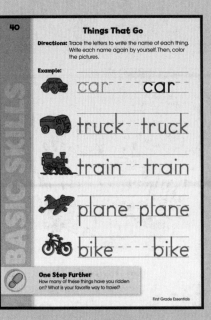	Sunday
	Monday
Tuesday	Tuesday
Saturday	Wednesday
Monday	
Friday	Thursday
Thursday	Friday
Sunday	
Wednesday	Saturday

One Step Further
What is your favorite day of the week? What do you like about it?

First Grade Essentials

37

Months of the Year

The months of the year begin with capital letters.

Directions: Write the months of the year in order on the calendar below. Be sure to start with capital letters.

January	December	April	May
October	June	September	February
July	March	November	August

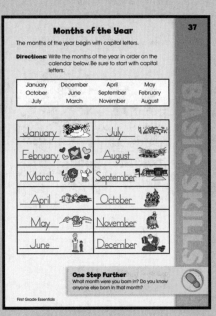

January	July
February	August
March	September
April	October
May	November
June	December

One Step Further
What month were you born in? Do you know anyone else born in that month?

First Grade Essentials

38

Color Names

Directions: Trace the letters to write the name of each color. Then, write the name again by yourself.

Example:

orange orange

blue blue

green green

yellow yellow

red red

brown brown

One Step Further
Find an object in your home that matches each color on this page.

First Grade Essentials

39

Number Words

Directions: Trace the letters to write the name of each number. Then, color the number pictures.

1 one   **2** two

3 three   **4** four

5 five   **6** six

7 seven   **8** eight

9 nine   **10** ten

One Step Further
How old are you? Circle that number. Draw a birthday cake with candles.

First Grade Essentials

40

Things That Go

Directions: Trace the letters to write the name of each thing. Write each name again by yourself. Then, color the pictures.

Example:

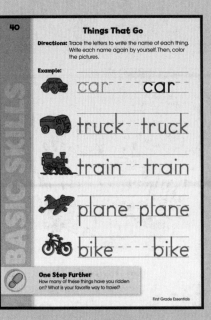

car car

truck truck

train train

plane plane

bike bike

One Step Further
How many of these things have you ridden on? What is your favorite way to travel?

First Grade Essentials

41

Food Names

Directions: Trace the letters to write the name of each food. Write each name again by yourself. Then, color the pictures.

Example:

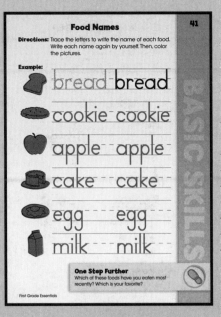

bread bread

cookie cookie

apple apple

cake cake

egg egg

milk milk

One Step Further
Which of these foods have you eaten most recently? Which is your favorite?

First Grade Essentials

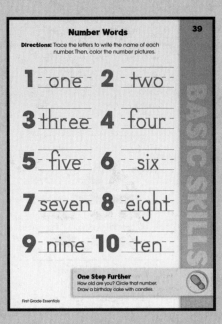

First Grade Essentials

ANSWER KEY

---

42 Riddles

Directions: Draw a line from the riddle to the animal it tells about.

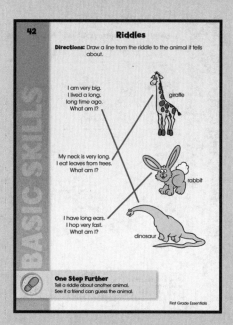

I am very big. I lived a long, long time ago. What am I? — giraffe

My neck is very long. I eat leaves from trees. What am I? — rabbit

I have long ears. I hop very fast. What am I? — dinosaur

One Step Further
Tell a riddle about another animal. See if a friend can guess the animal.

First Grade Essentials

BASIC SKILLS

---

43 Riddles

Directions: Write a word from the box to answer each riddle.

| sundae | book | chair | sun |

There are many words in me. I am fun to read. What am I?
book

I am soft and yellow. You can sit on me. What am I?
chair

I am in the sky in the day. I am hot. I am yellow. What am I?
sun

I am cold. I am sweet. You like to eat me. What am I?
sundae

One Step Further
Choose an object at school. Describe the object and ask a friend to guess.

First Grade Essentials

BASIC SKILLS

---

44 Zoo Animal Riddles

Directions: Write the name of the animal that answers each riddle.

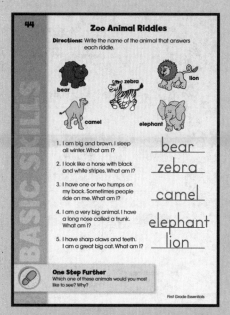

bear, zebra, lion, camel, elephant

1. I am big and brown. I sleep all winter. What am I?
bear

2. I look like a horse with black and white stripes. What am I?
zebra

3. I have one or two humps on my back. Sometimes people ride on me. What am I?
camel

4. I am a very big animal. I have a long nose called a trunk. What am I?
elephant

5. I have sharp claws and teeth. I am a great big cat. What am I?
lion

One Step Further
Which one of these animals would you most like to see? Why?

First Grade Essentials

BASIC SKILLS

---

46 Beginning Consonants: Bb, Cc, Dd, Ff

Consonants are the letters **b, c, d, f, g, h, j, k, l, m, n, p, q, r, s, t, v, w, x, y,** and **z.** Many words begin with consonants.

Directions: Say the name of each letter. Say the sound each letter makes. Circle the letters that make the beginning sound for each picture.

Bb   Cc   Dd   Ff

Bb (Dd)   (Ff) Cc   Cc (Dd)   (Ff) Bb

(Bb) Dd   (Ff) Cc   (Cc) Dd   Ff (Bb)

One Step Further
Name a friend or family member whose name starts with the **Bb** sound.

First Grade Essentials

READING

---

47 Beginning Consonants: Bb, Cc, Dd, Ff

Directions: Say the name of each letter. Say the sound each letter makes. Draw a line from each letter to the picture that begins with that sound.

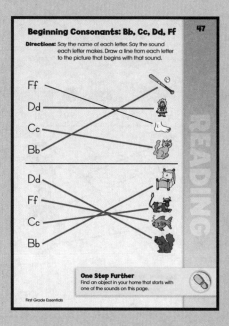

Ff
Dd
Cc
Bb

Dd
Ff
Cc
Bb

One Step Further
Find an object in your home that starts with one of the sounds on this page.

First Grade Essentials

READING

---

48 Beginning Consonants: Gg, Hh, Jj, Kk

Directions: Say the name of each letter. Say the sound each letter makes. Trace the letter pair that makes the beginning sound in each picture.

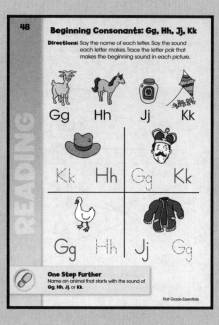

Gg   Hh   Jj   Kk

Kk   Hh   Gg   Kk

Gg   Hh   Jj   Gg

One Step Further
Name an animal that starts with the sound of **Gg, Hh, Jj,** or **Kk.**

First Grade Essentials

READING

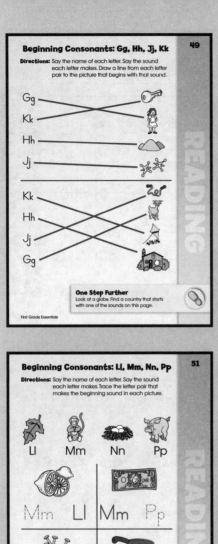

Beginning Consonants: Gg, Hh, Jj, Kk — 49

Directions: Say the name of each letter. Say the sound each letter makes. Draw a line from each letter pair to the picture that begins with that sound.

Gg
Kk
Hh
Jj

Kk
Hh
Jj
Gg

One Step Further
Look at a globe. Find a country that starts with one of the sounds on this page.

First Grade Essentials

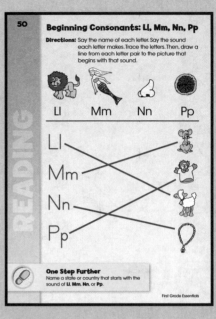

50 — **Beginning Consonants: Ll, Mm, Nn, Pp**

Directions: Say the name of each letter. Say the sound each letter makes. Trace the letters. Then, draw a line from each letter pair to the picture that begins with that sound.

Ll   Mm   Nn   Pp

Ll
Mm
Nn
Pp

One Step Further
Name a state or country that starts with the sound of **Ll, Mm, Nn,** or **Pp.**

First Grade Essentials

Beginning Consonants: Ll, Mm, Nn, Pp — 51

Directions: Say the name of each letter. Say the sound each letter makes. Trace the letter pair that makes the beginning sound in each picture.

Ll   Mm   Nn   Pp

Mm | Ll | Mm | Pp

Ll | Nn | Pp | Mm

One Step Further
Draw a map of your state. Mark the city where you live in the right spot on the map.

First Grade Essentials

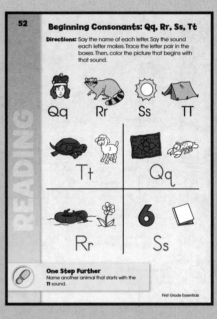

52 — **Beginning Consonants: Qq, Rr, Ss, Tt**

Directions: Say the name of each letter. Say the sound each letter makes. Trace the letter pair in the boxes. Then, color the picture that begins with that sound.

Qq   Rr   Ss   TT

Tt | Qq

Rr | Ss

One Step Further
Name another animal that starts with the **Tt** sound.

First Grade Essentials

Beginning Consonants: Qq, Rr, Ss, Tt — 53

Directions: Say the name of each letter. Say the sound each letter makes. Draw a line from each letter pair to the picture that begins with that sound.

Qq
Ss
Rr
Tt

Tt
Ss
Rr
Qq

One Step Further
Find an object in your school that starts with one of the sounds on this page.

First Grade Essentials

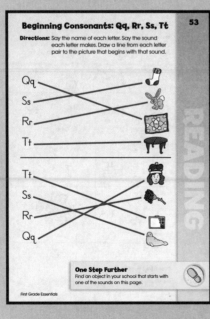

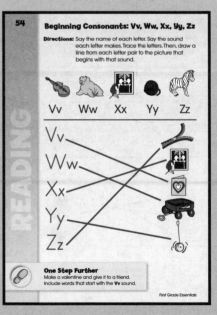

54 — **Beginning Consonants: Vv, Ww, Xx, Yy, Zz**

Directions: Say the name of each letter. Say the sound each letter makes. Trace the letters. Then, draw a line from each letter pair to the picture that begins with that sound.

Vv   Ww   Xx   Yy   Zz

Vv
Ww
Xx
Yy
Zz

One Step Further
Make a valentine and give it to a friend. Include words that start with the **Vv** sound.

First Grade Essentials

229

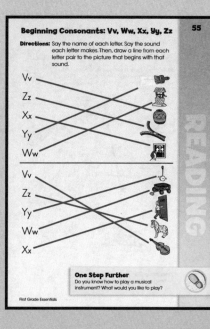

55 — Beginning Consonants: Vv, Ww, Xx, Yy, Zz
Directions: Say the name of each letter. Say the sound each letter makes. Then, draw a line from each letter pair to the picture that begins with that sound.

One Step Further
Do you know how to play a musical instrument? What would you like to play?

First Grade Essentials

56 — Ending Consonants: b, d, f
Directions: Say the name of each picture. Then, write the letter that makes the ending sound for each picture.

One Step Further
What sound does your first name end with? What sound does your last name end with?

First Grade Essentials

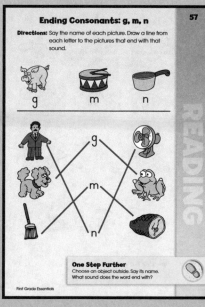

57 — Ending Consonants: g, m, n
Directions: Say the name of each picture. Draw a line from each letter to the pictures that end with that sound.

One Step Further
Choose an object outside. Say its name. What sound does the word end with?

First Grade Essentials

58 — Ending Consonants: k, l, p
Directions: Trace the letter in each row. Say the name of each picture. Then, color the pictures in each row that end with that sound.

One Step Further
How many of the objects on this page can you find in your home?

First Grade Essentials

59 — Ending Consonants: r, s, t, x
Directions: Say the name of each picture. Then, circle the ending sound for each picture.

One Step Further
Ask a friend to name several objects. What is the ending sound for each word?

First Grade Essentials

60 — Make a New Word
Directions: Write the beginning letter of each word in the boxes to make a new word.

1. c a p
2. s u n
3. t e n
4. s i t
5. r u g

One Step Further
Make a list of as many three-letter words as you can. How many did you list?

First Grade Essentials

First Grade Essentials

More New Words

61

Directions: Write the beginning letter of each word in the boxes to make a new word.

1. h a n d
2. 10 a n t
3. p o t
4. p l l a y
5. y a k

Directions: Write the first letter of each word you wrote to find the mystery word.

h a p p y

One Step Further
Name five things you do that make you happy. Then, go do one of them.

First Grade Essentials

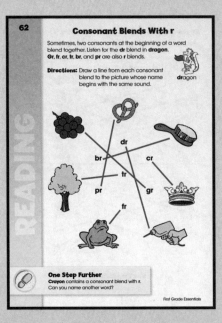

62 ### Consonant Blends With r

Sometimes, two consonants at the beginning of a word blend together. Listen for the **dr** blend in **dragon**. **Gr, fr, cr, tr, br,** and **pr** are also **r** blends.

Directions: Draw a line from each consonant blend to the picture whose name begins with the same sound.

dragon

dr
br   cr
          tr
pr   gr
     fr

One Step Further
Crayon contains a consonant blend with r. Can you name another word?

First Grade Essentials

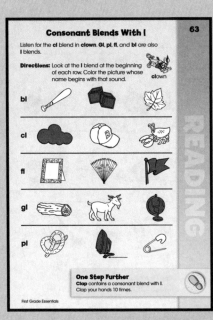

Consonant Blends With l

63

Listen for the **cl** blend in **clown**. **Gl, pl, fl,** and **bl** are also **l** blends.

Directions: Look at the **l** blend at the beginning of each row. Color the picture whose name begins with that sound.

clown

bl
cl
fl
gl
pl

One Step Further
Clap contains a consonant blend with l. Clap your hands 10 times.

First Grade Essentials

64 ### Consonant Blends With s

Listen for the **sk** blend in **skunk**. **Sm, st, sp, sw, sc, squ, sl,** and **sn** are also **s** blends.

Directions: Say the name of each picture. Circle the **s** blend you hear at the beginning of the name.

skunk

sn sp st / sw squ sl / squ st sp
st sp sk / sc sm / squ sc st
sw sl sm / sm sk / squ sn sm

One Step Further
Draw a snake. Draw a spoon. What consonant blends do those words contain?

First Grade Essentials

Blends at the Ends

65

Some consonant blends come at the ends of words. Listen for the **nd** blend at the end of the word **round**. **Mp, ng, nt, sk, nk,** and **st** can also be ending blends.

Directions: Say the name of each picture. Circle the blend you hear at the end of the name.

round

nd st sk / nt nk ng / nt st nd
nd ng mp / ng nt nd / nd nk st
st nt nd / nd nk ng / nt sk st

One Step Further
Be very quiet and listen closely. What sounds can you hear around you?

First Grade Essentials

66 ### Meet Short a

Listen for the sound of short **a** in **van**.

Directions: Trace the letter. Write it on the line.

van

A A A A A A

a a a a a a

Directions: Color the pictures whose names have the short **a** sound.

One Step Further
How many words can you name that rhyme with **cat**? Do they have the short **a** sound?

First Grade Essentials

Short a Maze
67

Directions: Help the cat get to the bag. Connect all the pictures whose names have the short **a** sound from the cat to the bag.

One Step Further
Draw more objects that have the short **a** sound.

First Grade Essentials

Meet Short e
68

Listen for the sound of short **e** in **hen**.

Directions: Trace the letter. Write it on the line. hen

E E E E E

e e e e e e

Directions: Color the pictures whose names have the short **e** sound.

One Step Further
Tell a story about a hen. What words in your story have the short **e** sound?

First Grade Essentials

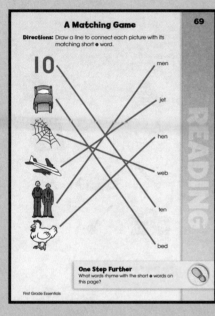

A Matching Game
69

Directions: Draw a line to connect each picture with its matching short **e** word.

men
jet
hen
web
ten
bed

One Step Further
What words rhyme with the short **e** words on this page?

First Grade Essentials

Meet Short i
70

Listen for the sound of short **i** in **pig**.

Directions: Trace the letter. Write it on the line. pig

I I I I I I

i i i i i i

Directions: Say the name of each picture. Color the trim on the bib if the name has the short **i** sound.

One Step Further
Name six words that have the short **i** sound. Think of rhyming words if you have to.

First Grade Essentials

Read and Color Short i
71

Directions: Say the name of each thing in the picture. Color the pictures whose names have the short **i** sound. The words in the box will give you hints.

| milk | crib | bib |
| pig | kitten | fish |

One Step Further
Tell a story about what is happening in the picture.

First Grade Essentials

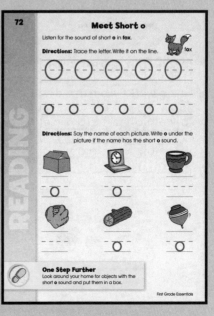

Meet Short o
72

Listen for the sound of short **o** in **fox**.

Directions: Trace the letter. Write it on the line. fox

O O O O O O

o o o o o o

Directions: Say the name of each picture. Write **o** under the picture if the name has the short **o** sound.

o   o   o

o   o   o

One Step Further
Look around your home for objects with the short **o** sound and put them in a box.

First Grade Essentials

First Grade Essentials

ANSWER KEY

READING

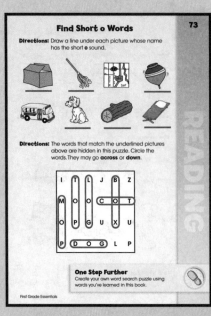

Find Short o Words

73

Directions: Draw a line under each picture whose name has the short **o** sound.

Directions: The words that match the underlined pictures above are hidden in this puzzle. Circle the words. They may go **across** or **down**.

I	T	L	J	B	Z
M	O	O	C	O	T
O	P	G	U	X	U
P	D	O	G	L	P

One Step Further
Create your own word search puzzle using words you've learned in this book.

First Grade Essentials

74

Meet Short u

Listen for the sound of short **u** in **bug**.

Directions: Trace the letter. Write it on the line.

U U U U U

u u u u u u

Directions: Say the name of each picture. Color the sun if you hear the short **u** sound in the name.

One Step Further
Snug as a bug in a rug! Snuggle under a blanket and read a book.

First Grade Essentials

Short u Tic-Tac-Toe

75

Directions: Color the pictures whose names have the short **u** sound. Then, play tic-tac-toe. Draw a line through three colored pictures in a row.

One Step Further
Play a game of tic-tac-toe with a friend. The winner should name a short **u** word.

First Grade Essentials

76

Meet Long a

Listen for the sound of long **a** in **cake**. Look for **a_e**.

Directions: Color the pictures whose names have the long **a** sound.

One Step Further
What vowels does your name contain? Are they long or short vowels?

First Grade Essentials

Words With Long a

77

Directions: Circle the words in the puzzle. The words go across and down.

p	a	p	e	r	z	l	a	m	n	o	b	c
t	s	l	x	a	c	r	a	y	o	n	d	a
u	z	p	w	d	q	y	b	n	m	p	e	v
m	v	y	r	i	q	p	e	o	a	k	l	l
a	v	e	b	o	r	z	l	z	g	a	m	e
y	c	r	a	z	y	a	r	e	p	a	y	f
b	w	s	b	b	x	t	o	d	a	y	j	g
e	t	c	y	y	v	a	c	a	t	i	o	n
h	i	g	h	w	a	y	l	a	z	y	h	i

paper	crayon
radio	maybe
crazy	today
baby	game
lazy	highway
vacation	repay

One Step Further
Draw more objects that have the long **a** sound.

First Grade Essentials

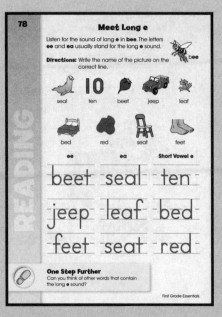

78

Meet Long e

Listen for the sound of long **e** in **bee**. The letters **ee** and **ea** usually stand for the long **e** sound.

Directions: Write the name of the picture on the correct line.

seal   ten   beet   jeep   leaf

bed   red   seat   feet

ee	ea	Short Vowel e
beet	seal	ten
jeep	leaf	bed
feet	seat	red

One Step Further
Can you think of other words that contain the long **e** sound?

First Grade Essentials

Page 79 — Words With Long e

Words With Long e 79

Directions: Circle the words in the puzzle. The words go across and down.

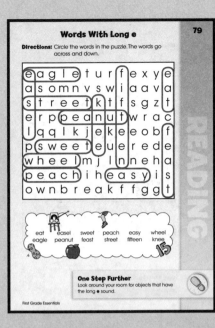

eat easel sweet peach easy wheel
eagle peanut feast street fifteen knee

One Step Further
Look around your room for objects that have the long **e** sound.

First Grade Essentials

Page 80 — Meet Long i

80 **Meet Long i**

Listen for the sound of long **i** in **bike**. Look for **i__e**.

Directions: Fill in the circle beside the name of the picture.

○ dim ● five ● kite
○ date ○ fix ○ cat
● dime ○ fame ○ kit

○ pane ○ tin ○ red
○ pin ○ tire ○ ride
● pine ○ tale ● rid

● hive ○ nip ○ fame
○ hid ○ name ● fire
○ had ● nine ○ fin

One Step Further
What words rhyme with the words you marked? Do they have the long **i** sound, too?

First Grade Essentials

Page 81 — Words With Long i

Words With Long i 81

Directions: Can you find nine hidden pictures of long-i words? Circle them.

🚲 bike   ✏ kite   🎵 nine
5 five   lime   pipe
hive   dime   slide

One Step Further
Name the other objects in the picture. What vowel sounds do they contain?

First Grade Essentials

Page 82 — Meet Long o

82 **Meet Long o**

Listen for the sound of long **o** in **rose**. Look for **o__e**.

Directions: Say the name of each picture. Decide whether the vowel sound you hear is long **o** or short **o**. Fill in the circle beside long **o** or short **o**.

● Long o   ○ Long o   ● Long o
○ Short o   ● Short o   ○ Short o

○ Long o   ○ Long o   ○ Long o
● Short o   ● Short o   ● Short o

● Long o   ○ Long o   ○ Long o
○ Short o   ● Short o   ● Short o

● Long o   ○ Long o   ○ Long o
○ Short o   ● Short o   ● Short o

One Step Further
Make up a story. Use at least four of the objects you see on this page.

First Grade Essentials

Page 83 — Words With Long o

Words With Long o 83

Directions: Circle the words in the puzzle. The words go across and down.

open   no   hero   globe
ocean   zero   echo   alone
poem   piano   home   phone

One Step Further
What do you think makes someone a hero? Do you have a hero?

First Grade Essentials

Page 84 — Meet Long u

84 **Meet Long u**

Listen for the sound of long **u** in **mule**. The letters **u__e** and **ue** usually stand for the long **u** sound.

Directions: Circle the pictures whose names have the long **u** sound.

One Step Further
Name your favorite color. What vowel sound does it contain?

First Grade Essentials

First Grade Essentials

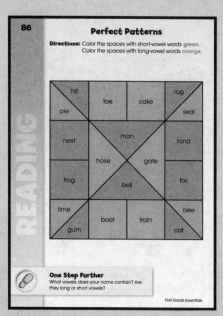

Words With Long u | 85

Directions: Circle the long-u word that matches each picture.

- (cute) / rule
- tube / dune
- (mule) / prune
- dude / (glue)
- Sue / (cube)
- fume / (June)
- (blue) / tune
- (flute) / rude

One Step Further
Choose a word you circled. Can you name three rhyming words?

First Grade Essentials

Perfect Patterns | 86

Directions: Color the spaces with short-vowel words green. Color the spaces with long-vowel words orange.

hit / pie	toe	cake	rug / seal
nest	man		land
	hose	gate	
frog	bell		fox
lime / gum	boat	train	bee / cat

One Step Further
What vowels does your name contain? Are they long or short vowels?

First Grade Essentials

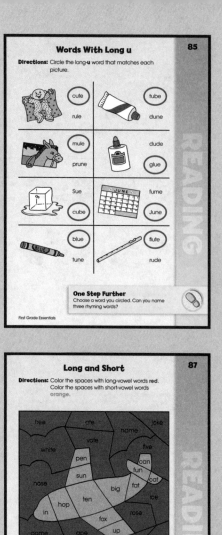

Long and Short | 87

Directions: Color the spaces with long-vowel words red. Color the spaces with short-vowel words orange.

tree, ate, joke, name, vote, white, five, pen, can, sun, fun, cat, nose, big, fat, ten, ice, in, hop, fox, rose, game, ape, up, home, note, came, wave, ride, plane, face

One Step Further
Have you ever traveled by plane? Where would you like to fly to?

First Grade Essentials

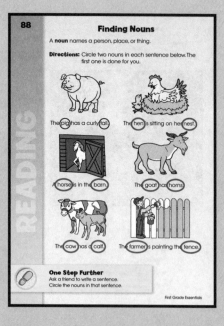

Finding Nouns | 88

A **noun** names a person, place, or thing.

Directions: Circle two nouns in each sentence below. The first one is done for you.

- The (pig) has a curly (tail).
- The (hen) is sitting on her (nest).
- A (horse) is in the (barn).
- The (goat) has horns.
- The (cow) has a (calf).
- The (farmer) is painting the (fence).

One Step Further
Ask a friend to write a sentence. Circle the nouns in that sentence.

First Grade Essentials

Person, Place, or Thing? | 89

Directions: Write each noun in the correct box below.

| girl | school | tree | truck | ball | zoo |
| artist | park | store | doctor | vase | baby |

Person
girl · artist · doctor · baby

Place
park · zoo · school · store

Thing
truck · vase · tree · ball

One Step Further
What other words could fit into the **Person** category?

First Grade Essentials

What Is a Verb? | 90

A **verb** is an action word. A verb tells what a person or thing does.

Example: Jane **reads** a book.

Directions: Circle the verb in each sentence below.

- Two tiny dogs (dance).
- The bear (climbs) a ladder.
- The clown (falls) down.
- A tiger (jumps) through a ring.
- A boy (eats) popcorn.
- A woman (swings) on a trapeze.

One Step Further
Name the first thing you do in the morning. What is the verb?

First Grade Essentials

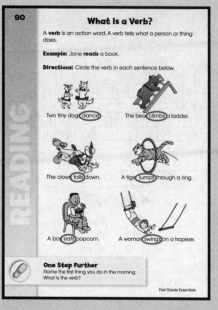

Ready, Set, Go! — 91

An **action word** tells what a person or thing can do.

Example: Fred **kicks** the ball.

Directions: Read the words below. Circle words that tell what the children are doing.

One Step Further
Draw a picture of a girl skating in the park.
Go outside and pretend you are skating!

First Grade Essentials

Words That Describe — 92

Directions: Read the words in the box. Choose the word that describes, or tells about, the picture. Write it next to the picture.

| wet | round | funny | soft | sad | tall |

One Step Further
Choose an object in your bedroom.
Use three words to describe it.

First Grade Essentials

Adjectives — 93

Describing words are also called **adjectives**.

Directions: Circle the describing words in the sentences.

1. The juicy apple is on the plate.
2. The furry dog is eating a bone.
3. It was a sunny day.
4. The kitten drinks warm milk.
5. The baby has a loud cry.

One Step Further
Describe your favorite subject in school.
What do you like about it?

First Grade Essentials

We're the Same! — 94

Words that mean the **same** thing, or close to the same thing, are called **synonyms**.

Directions: Write a word from the word box that has the same meaning as each word below.

| bright | hop | dad | fast |
| pretty | plate | silly | center |

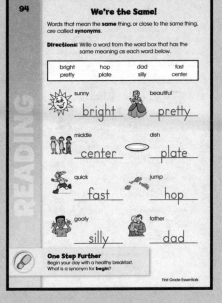

sunny — bright
beautiful — pretty
middle — center
dish — plate
quick — fast
jump — hop
goofy — silly
father — dad

One Step Further
Begin your day with a healthy breakfast.
What is a synonym for **begin**?

First Grade Essentials

Words and Meanings — 95

Directions: Read the two words on each dinosaur. If they have the same meaning, color the dinosaur green. If they do not have the same meaning, color the dinosaur red.

One Step Further
Write a sentence. Is there any word in your sentence you can replace with a synonym?

First Grade Essentials

Antonym Artists! — 96

Antonyms are words that have **opposite** meanings. Abby and Abe are Antonym Artists! They like to draw opposite pictures.

Directions: Help Abe draw the opposite of Abby's pictures.

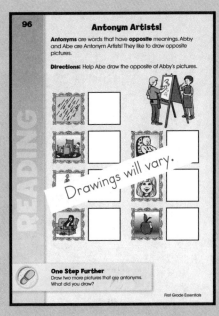

Drawings will vary.

One Step Further
Draw two more pictures that are antonyms.
What did you draw?

First Grade Essentials

First Grade Essentials

Antonyms are Opposites! — 97

Words with **opposite** meanings are called **antonyms**.

Directions: Circle an antonym for the underlined word in each sentence.

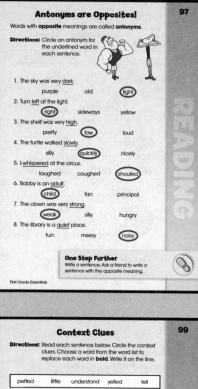

1. The sky was very dark.
   purple   old   (light)
2. Turn left at the light.
   (right)   sideways   yellow
3. The shelf was very high.
   pretty   (low)   loud
4. The turtle walked slowly.
   silly   (quickly)   nicely
5. I whispered at the circus.
   laughed   coughed   (shouted)
6. Bobby is an adult.
   (child)   fan   principal
7. The clown was very strong.
   (weak)   silly   hungry
8. The library is a quiet place.
   fun   messy   (noisy)

One Step Further
Write a sentence. Ask a friend to write a sentence with the opposite meaning.

First Grade Essentials

Context Clues — 98

Directions: Read each sentence below. Circle the context clues. Choose the answer that fits in each blank. Write it on the line.

1. The (cold) wind and lack of (heat) made me wish I had an extra __jacket__
   umbrella   toy   shovel   jacket
2. A whale is a very __large__ mammal. Sailors often thought whales were actually (small islands)
   small   graceful   large   blue
3. Eating fruit is important for __good__ health. Fruit is full of many important (vitamins)
   bad   good   okay   cat
4. The bus was (very large) and had (a lot) of seats. It could carry __many__ people.
   few   hungry   many   tired
5. The clown looked very __silly__ wearing a tiny pink (tutu!)
   silly   smart   orange   light

One Step Further
Name everything you do for good health. Do you eat fruit? Exercise?

First Grade Essentials

Context Clues — 99

Directions: Read each sentence below. Circle the context clues. Choose a word from the word list to replace each word in **bold**. Write it on the line.

| petted | little | understand | yelled | tell |

1. "Don't **reveal** the secret! We want the party to (be a surprise!) said Mary. __tell__
2. I can't **grasp** that (hard math problem.) It is too difficult. __understand__
3. The baby bird was so **tiny** that we could (hardly) (see it.) __little__
4. We **stroked** the (soft kitten) and heard it purr. __petted__
5. The crowd **hollered** when the player was (called out.) __yelled__

One Step Further
Do something to surprise a friend. Make your friend a card or give him or her a gift.

First Grade Essentials

Homonyms — 100

Homonyms are words that sound the same, but are spelled differently and have different meanings. For example, **sun** and **son** are homonyms.

Directions: Look at the word. Circle the picture that goes with the word.

1. sun
2. hi
3. ate
4. four
5. buy
6. hear

One Step Further
What was the last thing you ate? Name eight of your favorite foods.

First Grade Essentials

Homonyms — 101

Directions: Look at each picture. Circle the homonym that is spelled the correct way.

(deer) dear

blue (blew)

2
to (two)

hi (high)

by (bye)

(new) knew

8
ate (eight)

red (read)

One Step Further
What are the last two books you read? What were the books about?

First Grade Essentials

Batty Bats! — 102

Some words have more than one meaning. The word **bat** has more than one meaning.

Directions: Look at the words and their meanings below. Below each picture, write the number that has the correct meaning.

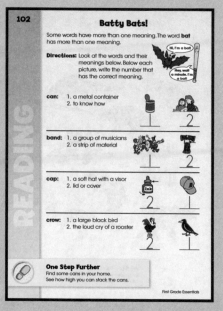

can: 1. a metal container
2. to know how

band: 1. a group of musicians
2. a strip of material

cap: 1. a soft hat with a visor
2. lid or cover

crow: 1. a large black bird
2. the loud cry of a rooster

One Step Further
Find some cans in your home. See how high you can stack the cans.

First Grade Essentials

First Grade Essentials

ANSWER KEY

Match That Meaning! 103

Some words have more than one meaning. Look at the list of words.

Directions: Match the word's correct meaning to the pictures below.

cross: 1. to draw a line through
            2. angry

fall: 3. the season between summer and winter
            4. to trip or stumble

land: 5. to bring to a stop or rest
            6. the ground

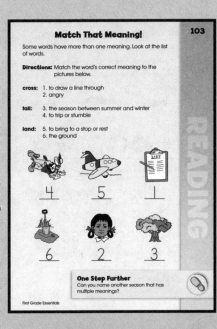

4   5   1

6   2   3

One Step Further
Can you name another season that has multiple meanings?

First Grade Essentials

---

104 Solve the Mystery

Directions: Read each sentence and cross out the picture. What picture is left?

1. It is not a tube.
2. It is not glue.
3. It is not an ice cube.
4. It is not a mule.
5. It is not June.
6. It is not blue.

The mystery picture is a ‗ ‗ flute ‗ ‗

One Step Further
What vowel sound is in all of these picture names? What other words have that sound?

First Grade Essentials

Solve the Mystery 105

Directions: Read each sentence and cross out the picture. What picture is left?

1. It is not a toy.
2. It is not foil.
3. It is not boil.
4. It is not coins.
5. It is not soil.
6. It is not oil.

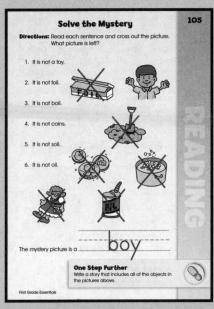

The mystery picture is a ‗ ‗ boy ‗ ‗

One Step Further
Write a story that includes all of the objects in the pictures above.

First Grade Essentials

---

106 Clues About Cats

Directions: Read the clues carefully. Then, number the cats. When you are sure you are correct, color the cats.

1. A gray cat sits on the gate.
2. A cat with orange-and-black spots sits near the tree.
3. A brown cat sits near the bush.
4. A [ ] cat sits between the orange-and-black spotted cat and the gray cat.
5. A black cat sits next to the brown cat.
6. An orange cat sits between the gray cat and the black cat.

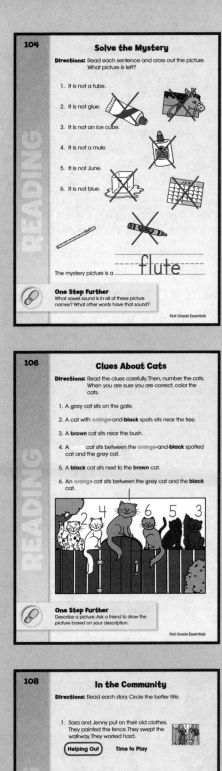

2 4 6 5 3

One Step Further
Describe a picture. Ask a friend to draw the picture based on your description.

First Grade Essentials

Critical Thinking 107

Directions: Use your reading skills to answer each riddle. Unscramble the word to check your answer. Write the correct word on the line.

I am a ruler, but I have two feet, not one.
I am a **king** (ngik)

I am very bright, but that doesn't make me smart.
I am the **sun** (uns)

You can turn me around, but I won't get dizzy.
I am a **key** (eky)

I can rattle, but I am not a baby's toy.
I am a **snake** (nekas)

I will give you milk, but not in a bottle.
I am a **cow** (ocw)

I smell, but I have no nose.
I am a **flower** (oerflw)

One Step Further
Tell these riddles to a friend.
Did your friend guess the riddles correctly?

First Grade Essentials

---

108 In the Community

Directions: Read each story. Circle the better title.

1. Sara and Jenny put on their old clothes. They painted the fence. They swept the walkway. They worked hard.
   Helping Out   Time to Play

2. The families took their old things to the park. They had a big sale. They gave the money to the Children's Center.
   Family Fun   **A Big Sale**

3. Happy Town had a big fair. There were games and rides for the kids. Everyone had a good time!
   Fun at the Fair   Time to Vote

4. Hill Town wanted its own community center. The people raised money. When they had enough, they built the center.
   Our Community Center   The Big Fire

One Step Further
Write a short story about what you did today. Give it the best title.

First Grade Essentials

Hey! What's the Big Idea? — 109

Directions: Circle the words that are shown in the picture above.

(bowl) pan scooter socks
oven (napkins) car (milk)
(mixer) paper (cat) ink
mitt towels dog phone
(spoon) bed pot sneakers
(spatula) jar (girl) (cupcake tin)

Directions: Circle and write the best title for the picture.

Baking With Dad (Chocolate Attack!) Eating Food

Chocolate Attack!

Tell why the other two titles are not as good.

They aren't as clever or as interesting.

One Step Further
Ask an adult to help you bake cupcakes.
Describe the steps you take.

First Grade Essentials

Fish Come in Many Colors — 110

Directions: Read about the color of fish. Then, color the fish.

Many fish live in this lake. Fish that live at the top are blue, green, or **black**. Fish that live down deep are silver or red. The colors help the fish hide in the lake.

1. Name three colors of fish that live at the top.

blue green black

2. Name two colors of fish that live down deep.

red silver

3. Color the top fish and the bottom fish the correct colors.

One Step Further
Is there a fish tank in your home or school?
What color are the fish that live there?

First Grade Essentials

Boats — 111

Directions: Read about boats. Then, answer the questions.

See the boats! They float on water. Some boats have sails. The wind moves the sails. It makes the boats go. Many people name their sailboats. They paint the name on the side of the boat.

1. What makes sailboats move? **wind**

2. Where do sailboats float? **water**

3. What would you name a sailboat? **Answers will vary.**

One Step Further
Have you ever been on a boat?
Tell a story about riding on a boat.

First Grade Essentials

Story Time — 112

The **main idea** tells about the **whole story**.

Read the story below.

"Mom, can we build a fort in the dining room?" John asked.
"Sure, honey," said John's mom. Then, John's mom covered the dining room table with a giant sheet. "Do you want to eat lunch in our fort?" asked John's mom.
"Yes!" said John. Then, John's mom brought two peanut butter sandwiches on paper plates and sat under the table, too!
"Mom, making a fort with you is so much fun!" said John, smiling.

Directions: Does the sentence tell the main idea? Write **yes** or **no**.

1. Then, John's mom covered the dining room table with a giant sheet. **no**

2. "Do you want to eat lunch in our fort?" asked John's mom. **no**

3. "Mom, making a fort with you is so much fun!" **yes**

4. Write a sentence that tells the main idea: **John and his mom made a fort.**

One Step Further
With a friend, build a fort somewhere in your home. What will you do in your fort?

First Grade Essentials

Sums 0 to 3 — 114

Directions: Add.

$\frac{1}{+1}{2}$

$1 + 1 = \underline{2}$

$2 + 1 = \underline{3}$

$\frac{2}{+1}{3}$

$1 + 2 = \underline{3}$

$\frac{1}{+2}{3}$

$2 + 0 = \underline{2}$

$\frac{2}{+0}{2}$

$3 + 0 = \underline{3}$

$\frac{3}{+0}{3}$

$0 + 2 = \underline{2}$

$\frac{0}{+2}{2}$

$0 + 3 = \underline{3}$

$\frac{0}{+3}{3}$

$0 + 0 = \underline{0}$

$\frac{0}{+0}{0}$

$1 + 0 = \underline{1}$

$\frac{1}{+0}{1}$

$0 + 1 = \underline{1}$

$\frac{0}{+1}{1}$

One Step Further
Find two pencils. Find one crayon.
Add how many objects there are.

First Grade Essentials

Sums of 4 and 5 — 115

Directions: Add.

$\frac{4}{+1}{5}$

$4 + 1 = \underline{5}$

$2 + 3 = \underline{5}$

$\frac{2}{+3}{5}$

$\frac{1}{+4}{5}$

$1 + 4 = \underline{5}$

$3 + 2 = \underline{5}$

$\frac{3}{+2}{5}$

$\frac{2}{+2}{4}$

$2 + 2 = \underline{4}$

$4 + 0 = \underline{4}$

$\frac{4}{+0}{4}$

$0 + 4 = \underline{4}$

$\frac{0}{+4}{4}$

$\frac{5}{+0}{5}$

$5 + 0 = \underline{5}$

$1 + 3 = \underline{4}$

$\frac{1}{+3}{4}$

$\frac{0}{+5}{5}$

$0 + 5 = \underline{5}$

$3 + 1 = \underline{4}$

$\frac{3}{+1}{4}$

One Step Further
Find four buttons. Find one shirt.
Add how many objects there are.

First Grade Essentials

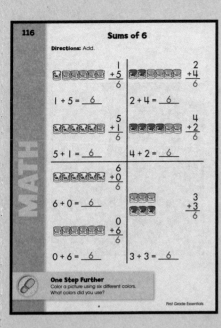

116 · Sums of 6
Directions: Add.

$1+5=\underline{6}$ $2+4=\underline{6}$
$5+1=\underline{6}$ $4+2=\underline{6}$
$6+0=\underline{6}$ $3+3=\underline{6}$
$0+6=\underline{6}$

One Step Further
Color a picture using six different colors. What colors did you use?

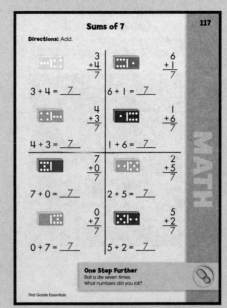

117 · Sums of 7
Directions: Add.

$3+4=\underline{7}$ $6+1=\underline{7}$
$4+3=\underline{7}$ $1+6=\underline{7}$
$7+0=\underline{7}$ $2+5=\underline{7}$
$0+7=\underline{7}$ $5+2=\underline{7}$

One Step Further
Roll a die seven times. What numbers did you roll?

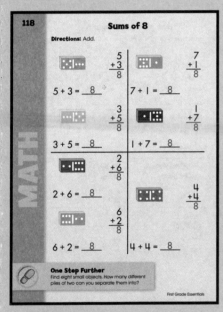

118 · Sums of 8
Directions: Add.

$5+3=\underline{8}$ $7+1=\underline{8}$
$3+5=\underline{8}$ $1+7=\underline{8}$
$2+6=\underline{8}$ $4+4=\underline{8}$
$6+2=\underline{8}$

One Step Further
Find eight small objects. How many different piles of two can you separate them into?

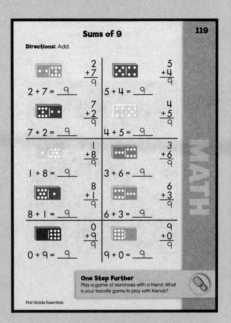

119 · Sums of 9
Directions: Add.

$2+7=\underline{9}$ $5+4=\underline{9}$
$7+2=\underline{9}$ $4+5=\underline{9}$
$1+8=\underline{9}$ $3+6=\underline{9}$
$8+1=\underline{9}$ $6+3=\underline{9}$
$0+9=\underline{9}$ $9+0=\underline{9}$

One Step Further
Play a game of dominoes with a friend. What is your favorite game to play with friends?

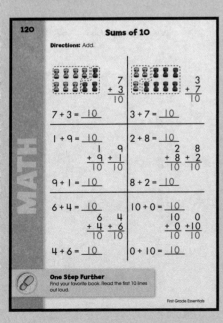

120 · Sums of 10
Directions: Add.

$7+3=\underline{10}$ $3+7=\underline{10}$
$1+9=\underline{10}$ $2+8=\underline{10}$
$9+1=\underline{10}$ $8+2=\underline{10}$
$6+4=\underline{10}$ $10+0=\underline{10}$
$4+6=\underline{10}$ $0+10=\underline{10}$

One Step Further
Find your favorite book. Read the first 10 lines out loud.

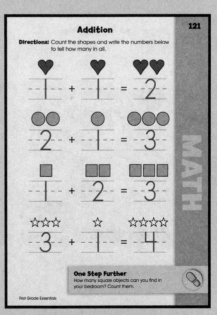

121 · Addition
Directions: Count the shapes and write the numbers below to tell how many in all.

$1+1=2$
$2+1=3$
$1+2=3$
$3+1=4$

One Step Further
How many square objects can you find in your bedroom? Count them.

ANSWER KEY

122

Farmers Need This

Directions: Add. Use the code to color the picture.

8 = red   9 = green   10 = black   12 = blue

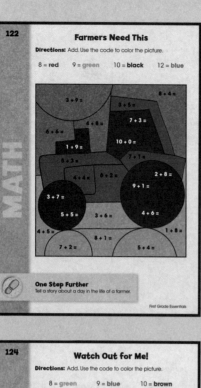

One Step Further
Tell a story about a day in the life of a farmer.

First Grade Essentials

123

What Is It?

Directions: Add. Use the code to color the picture.

6 = yellow   7 = purple   8 = blue

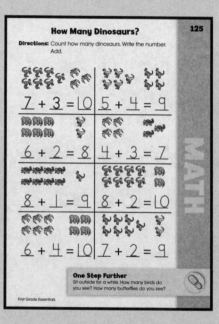

One Step Further
Draw a picture of another object using the colors yellow, purple, and blue.

First Grade Essentials

124

Watch Out for Me!

Directions: Add. Use the code to color the picture.

8 = green   9 = blue   10 = brown

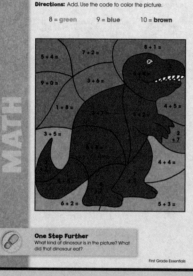

One Step Further
What kind of dinosaur is in the picture? What did that dinosaur eat?

First Grade Essentials

125

How Many Dinosaurs?

Directions: Count how many dinosaurs. Write the number. Add.

$7 + 3 = 10$ $5 + 4 = 9$

$6 + 2 = 8$ $4 + 3 = 7$

$8 + 1 = 9$ $8 + 2 = 10$

$6 + 4 = 10$ $7 + 2 = 9$

One Step Further
Sit outside for a while. How many birds do you see? How many butterflies do you see?

First Grade Essentials

126

Air Bear Addition

Directions: Help Buddy off the ground. Add to find the sum. Then, color the clouds with sums of 9 to find the right path.

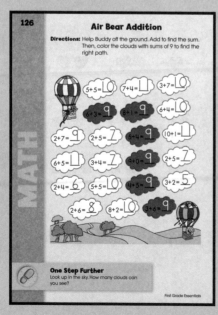

$5+5 = 10$ $7+4 = 11$ $3+7 = 10$
$6+3 = 9$ $8+1 = 9$ $6+4 = 10$
$2+7 = 9$ $2+5 = 7$ $6+4 = 9$ $10+1 = 11$
$6+5 = 11$ $3+4 = 7$ $9+0 = 9$ $2+5 = 7$
$2+4 = 6$ $5+5 = 10$ $4+5 = 9$ $3+2 = 5$
$2+6 = 8$ $8+2 = 10$ $3+6 = 9$

One Step Further
Look up in the sky. How many clouds can you see?

First Grade Essentials

127

Practicing Addition

Directions: Add.

$\begin{array}{r}6\\+4\\\hline10\end{array}$ $\begin{array}{r}7\\+2\\\hline9\end{array}$ $\begin{array}{r}4\\+4\\\hline8\end{array}$ $\begin{array}{r}4\\+5\\\hline9\end{array}$ $\begin{array}{r}9\\+1\\\hline10\end{array}$

$\begin{array}{r}2\\+7\\\hline9\end{array}$ $\begin{array}{r}6\\+2\\\hline8\end{array}$ $\begin{array}{r}9\\+0\\\hline9\end{array}$ $\begin{array}{r}2\\+5\\\hline7\end{array}$ $\begin{array}{r}1\\+4\\\hline5\end{array}$

$\begin{array}{r}8\\+1\\\hline9\end{array}$ $\begin{array}{r}2\\+2\\\hline4\end{array}$ $\begin{array}{r}3\\+6\\\hline9\end{array}$ $\begin{array}{r}1\\+7\\\hline8\end{array}$ $\begin{array}{r}7\\+3\\\hline10\end{array}$

$\begin{array}{r}2\\+3\\\hline5\end{array}$ $\begin{array}{r}2\\+8\\\hline10\end{array}$ $\begin{array}{r}3\\+5\\\hline8\end{array}$ $\begin{array}{r}8\\+2\\\hline10\end{array}$ $\begin{array}{r}6\\+1\\\hline7\end{array}$

$\begin{array}{r}1\\+9\\\hline10\end{array}$ $\begin{array}{r}6\\+3\\\hline9\end{array}$ $\begin{array}{r}3\\+4\\\hline7\end{array}$ $\begin{array}{r}5\\+2\\\hline7\end{array}$ $\begin{array}{r}5\\+4\\\hline9\end{array}$

One Step Further
What two numbers add up to equal your age?

First Grade Essentials

ANSWER KEY

---

128 — Problem Solving

Directions: Solve each problem.

There are five white [butterfly].
There are four blue [butterflies].
How many in all?
$$\begin{array}{r} 5 \\ +4 \\ \hline 9 \end{array}$$

There are three [sheep].
Seven more [sheep] come.
How many are there now?
$$\begin{array}{r} 3 \\ +7 \\ \hline 10 \end{array}$$

Beth has nine [shirt].
She buys one more.
Now how many does she have?
$$\begin{array}{r} 9 \\ +1 \\ \hline 10 \end{array}$$

There are six [candle].
There are three [candle].
How many in all?
$$\begin{array}{r} 6 \\ +3 \\ \hline 9 \end{array}$$

There were eight [dog].
Two more came.
Then how many were there?
$$\begin{array}{r} 8 \\ +2 \\ \hline 10 \end{array}$$

One Step Further
How many T-shirts do you own? How many
would you own if you bought one more?

First Grade Essentials

---

129 — Plenty to Wear!

Directions: The key words **in all** tell you to add. Circle the
key words **in all**. Write a sign in each problem
and solve.

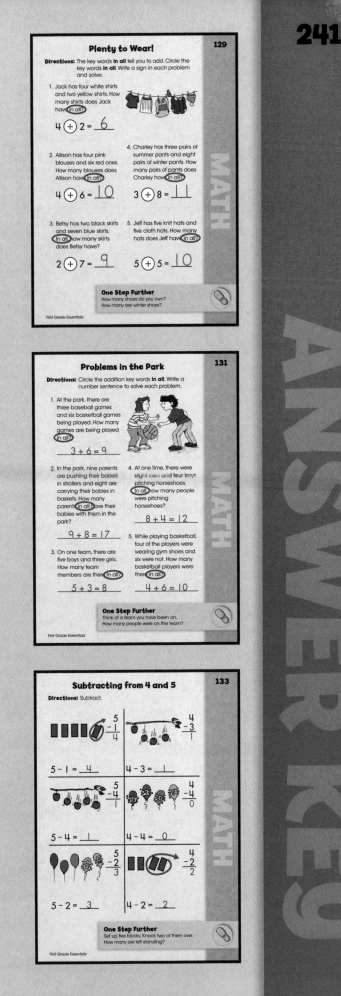

1. Jack has four white shirts
and two yellow shirts. How
many shirts does Jack
have (in all?)

$4 (+) 2 = 6$

2. Allison has four pink
blouses and six red ones.
How many blouses does
Allison have (in all?)

$4 (+) 6 = 10$

3. Betsy has two black skirts
and seven blue skirts.
(In all,) how many skirts
does Betsy have?

$2 (+) 7 = 9$

4. Charley has three pairs of
summer pants and eight
pairs of winter pants. How
many pairs of pants does
Charley have (in all?)

$3 (+) 8 = 11$

5. Jeff has five knit hats and
five cloth hats. How many
hats does Jeff have (in all?)

$5 (+) 5 = 10$

One Step Further
How many shoes do you own?
How many are winter shoes?

First Grade Essentials

---

130 — Solving Stories

Directions: Write a number sentence to solve each
problem.

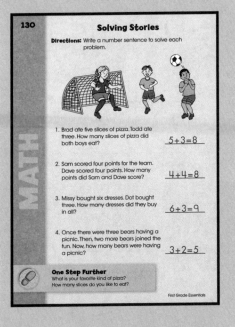

1. Brad ate five slices of pizza. Todd ate
three. How many slices of pizza did
both boys eat?

$5 + 3 = 8$

2. Sam scored four points for the team.
Dave scored four points. How many
points did Sam and Dave score?

$4 + 4 = 8$

3. Missy bought six dresses. Dot bought
three. How many dresses did they buy
in all?

$6 + 3 = 9$

4. Once there were three bears having a
picnic. Then, two more bears joined the
fun. Now, how many bears were having
a picnic?

$3 + 2 = 5$

One Step Further
What is your favorite kind of pizza?
How many slices do you like to eat?

First Grade Essentials

---

131 — Problems in the Park

Directions: Circle the addition key words **in all**. Write a
number sentence to solve each problem.

1. At the park, there are
three baseball games
and six basketball games
being played. How many
games are being played
(in all?)

$3 + 6 = 9$

2. In the park, nine parents
are pushing their babies
in strollers and eight are
carrying their babies in
baskets. How many
parents (in all) have their
babies with them in the
park?

$9 + 8 = 17$

3. On one team, there are
five boys and three girls.
How many team
members are there (in all?)

$5 + 3 = 8$

4. At one time, there were
eight men and four boys
pitching horseshoes.
(In all,) how many people
were pitching
horseshoes?

$8 + 4 = 12$

5. While playing basketball,
four of the players were
wearing gym shoes and
six were not. How many
basketball players were
there (in all?)

$4 + 6 = 10$

One Step Further
Think of a team you have been on.
How many people were on the team?

First Grade Essentials

---

132 — Subtracting from 1, 2, and 3

Directions: Subtract.

$$\begin{array}{r} 3 \\ -1 \\ \hline 2 \end{array}$$
$3 - 1 = 2$

$$\begin{array}{r} 2 \\ -1 \\ \hline 1 \end{array}$$
$2 - 1 = 1$

$$\begin{array}{r} 3 \\ -2 \\ \hline 1 \end{array}$$
$3 - 2 = 1$

$$\begin{array}{r} 1 \\ -0 \\ \hline 1 \end{array}$$
$1 - 0 = 1$

$$\begin{array}{r} 3 \\ -0 \\ \hline 3 \end{array}$$
$3 - 0 = 3$

$$\begin{array}{r} 1 \\ -1 \\ \hline 0 \end{array}$$
$1 - 1 = 0$

$$\begin{array}{r} 2 \\ -2 \\ \hline 0 \end{array}$$
$2 - 2 = 0$

$$\begin{array}{r} 3 \\ -3 \\ \hline 0 \end{array}$$
$3 - 3 = 0$

One Step Further
How many birds can you see out
your window?

First Grade Essentials

---

133 — Subtracting from 4 and 5

Directions: Subtract.

$$\begin{array}{r} 5 \\ -1 \\ \hline 4 \end{array}$$
$5 - 1 = 4$

$$\begin{array}{r} 4 \\ -3 \\ \hline 1 \end{array}$$
$4 - 3 = 1$

$$\begin{array}{r} 5 \\ -4 \\ \hline 1 \end{array}$$
$5 - 4 = 1$

$$\begin{array}{r} 4 \\ -4 \\ \hline 0 \end{array}$$
$4 - 4 = 0$

$$\begin{array}{r} 5 \\ -2 \\ \hline 3 \end{array}$$
$5 - 2 = 3$

$$\begin{array}{r} 4 \\ -2 \\ \hline 2 \end{array}$$
$4 - 2 = 2$

One Step Further
Set up five blocks. Knock two of them over.
How many are left standing?

First Grade Essentials

First Grade Essentials

ANSWER KEY

---

134 — **Subtracting from 6**

Directions: Subtract.

$\begin{array}{r} 6 \\ -1 \\ \hline 5 \end{array}$ $\begin{array}{r} 6 \\ -5 \\ \hline 1 \end{array}$

6 − 1 = __5__   6 − 5 = __1__

$\begin{array}{r} 6 \\ -4 \\ \hline 2 \end{array}$ $\begin{array}{r} 6 \\ -2 \\ \hline 4 \end{array}$

6 − 4 = __2__   6 − 2 = __4__

$\begin{array}{r} 6 \\ -3 \\ \hline 3 \end{array}$ $\begin{array}{r} 6 \\ -0 \\ \hline 6 \end{array}$

6 − 3 = __3__   6 − 0 = __6__

One Step Further
Draw six flowers for the bees to land on.
Color each flower a different color.

First Grade Essentials

---

135 — **Subtracting from 7**

Directions: Subtract.

$\begin{array}{r} 7 \\ -6 \\ \hline 1 \end{array}$ $\begin{array}{r} 7 \\ -1 \\ \hline 6 \end{array}$

7 − 6 = __1__   7 − 1 = __6__

$\begin{array}{r} 7 \\ -3 \\ \hline 4 \end{array}$ $\begin{array}{r} 7 \\ -4 \\ \hline 3 \end{array}$

7 − 3 = __4__   7 − 4 = __3__

$\begin{array}{r} 7 \\ -7 \\ \hline 0 \end{array}$ $\begin{array}{r} 7 \\ -0 \\ \hline 7 \end{array}$

7 − 7 = __0__   7 − 0 = __7__

$\begin{array}{r} 7 \\ -2 \\ \hline 5 \end{array}$ $\begin{array}{r} 7 \\ -5 \\ \hline 2 \end{array}$

7 − 2 = __5__   7 − 5 = __2__

One Step Further
Name the seven days of the week.
What day is your favorite?

First Grade Essentials

---

136 — **Subtracting from 8**

Directions: Subtract.

$\begin{array}{r} 8 \\ -7 \\ \hline 1 \end{array}$ $\begin{array}{r} 8 \\ -1 \\ \hline 7 \end{array}$

8 − 7 = __1__   8 − 1 = __7__

$\begin{array}{r} 8 \\ -2 \\ \hline 6 \end{array}$ $\begin{array}{r} 8 \\ -6 \\ \hline 2 \end{array}$

8 − 2 = __6__   8 − 6 = __2__

$\begin{array}{r} 8 \\ -4 \\ \hline 4 \end{array}$ $\begin{array}{r} 8 \\ -8 \\ \hline 0 \end{array}$

8 − 4 = __4__   8 − 8 = __0__

$\begin{array}{r} 8 \\ -3 \\ \hline 5 \end{array}$ $\begin{array}{r} 8 \\ -5 \\ \hline 3 \end{array}$

8 − 3 = __5__   8 − 5 = __3__

One Step Further
Can you name at least eight states?
What state do you live in?

First Grade Essentials

---

137 — **Subtracting from 9**

Directions: Subtract.

$\begin{array}{r} 9 \\ -6 \\ \hline 3 \end{array}$ $\begin{array}{r} 9 \\ -3 \\ \hline 6 \end{array}$

9 − 6 = __3__   9 − 3 = __6__

$\begin{array}{r} 9 \\ -0 \\ \hline 9 \end{array}$ $\begin{array}{r} 9 \\ -9 \\ \hline 0 \end{array}$

9 − 0 = __9__   9 − 9 = __0__

$\begin{array}{r} 9 \\ -5 \\ \hline 4 \end{array}$ $\begin{array}{r} 9 \\ -4 \\ \hline 5 \end{array}$

9 − 5 = __4__   9 − 4 = __5__

$\begin{array}{r} 9 \\ -8 \\ \hline 1 \end{array}$ $\begin{array}{r} 9 \\ -1 \\ \hline 8 \end{array}$

9 − 8 = __1__   9 − 1 = __8__

One Step Further
Roll two dice. How many rolls do you make
until you roll a total of nine?

First Grade Essentials

---

138 — **Subtracting from 10**

Directions: Subtract.

$\begin{array}{r} 10 \\ -1 \\ \hline 9 \end{array}$ $\begin{array}{r} 10 \\ -9 \\ \hline 1 \end{array}$

10 − 1 = __9__   10 − 9 = __1__

10 − 7 = __3__   10 − 4 = __6__

$\begin{array}{r} 10 \\ -7 \\ \hline 3 \end{array}$ $\begin{array}{r} 10 \\ -3 \\ \hline 7 \end{array}$ $\begin{array}{r} 10 \\ -4 \\ \hline 6 \end{array}$ $\begin{array}{r} 10 \\ -6 \\ \hline 4 \end{array}$

10 − 3 = __7__   10 − 6 = __4__

10 − 8 = __2__

$\begin{array}{r} 10 \\ -8 \\ \hline 2 \end{array}$ $\begin{array}{r} 10 \\ -2 \\ \hline 8 \end{array}$ $\begin{array}{r} 10 \\ -0 \\ \hline 10 \end{array}$

10 − 2 = __8__   10 − 0 = __10__

One Step Further
Can you whistle? Try to whistle for 10 seconds
while standing on one foot.

First Grade Essentials

---

139 — **A Swinging Adventure**

Directions: Solve the subtraction problems.

$\begin{array}{r} 7 \\ -2 \\ \hline 5 \end{array}$ $\begin{array}{r} 6 \\ -3 \\ \hline 3 \end{array}$ $\begin{array}{r} 4 \\ -3 \\ \hline 1 \end{array}$ $\begin{array}{r} 3 \\ -2 \\ \hline 1 \end{array}$

$\begin{array}{r} 10 \\ -7 \\ \hline 3 \end{array}$ $\begin{array}{r} 7 \\ -1 \\ \hline 6 \end{array}$ $\begin{array}{r} 10 \\ -1 \\ \hline 9 \end{array}$ $\begin{array}{r} 7 \\ -4 \\ \hline 3 \end{array}$

$\begin{array}{r} 6 \\ -4 \\ \hline 2 \end{array}$ $\begin{array}{r} 8 \\ -4 \\ \hline 4 \end{array}$ $\begin{array}{r} 9 \\ -5 \\ \hline 4 \end{array}$ $\begin{array}{r} 8 \\ -1 \\ \hline 7 \end{array}$ $\begin{array}{r} 9 \\ -2 \\ \hline 7 \end{array}$

$\begin{array}{r} 9 \\ -6 \\ \hline 3 \end{array}$ $\begin{array}{r} 5 \\ -4 \\ \hline 1 \end{array}$ $\begin{array}{r} 10 \\ -6 \\ \hline 4 \end{array}$ $\begin{array}{r} 7 \\ -3 \\ \hline 4 \end{array}$ $\begin{array}{r} 4 \\ -2 \\ \hline 2 \end{array}$

$\begin{array}{r} 5 \\ -1 \\ \hline 4 \end{array}$ $\begin{array}{r} 9 \\ -5 \\ \hline 4 \end{array}$ $\begin{array}{r} 9 \\ -3 \\ \hline 6 \end{array}$ $\begin{array}{r} 8 \\ -5 \\ \hline 3 \end{array}$ $\begin{array}{r} 7 \\ -3 \\ \hline 4 \end{array}$

One Step Further
Get with a friend and put on a play about
Robin Hood.

First Grade Essentials

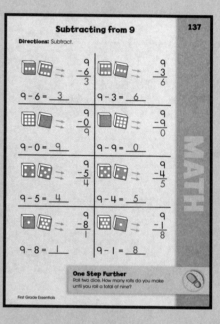

140

Subtracting

Six silly green frogs were sitting on six lily pads.

A big bird flew by and two frogs jumped off into the water.

Directions: Solve the subtraction problem by answering the questions.

How many frogs were sitting on the lily pads? __6__

How many frogs jumped off? __2__

How many frogs were left? __4__

One Step Further
Hop like a frog four times. How many birds can you see outside right now?

First Grade Essentials

141

Subtracting

Four hungry cats went on a picnic.

Two cats spotted some mice and took off to catch them!

Directions: Solve the subtraction problem by answering the questions.

How many cats went on the picnic? __4__

How many cats ran after the mice? __2__

How many cats were left? __2__

One Step Further
Tell a story about the cats' picnic. What happened before the mice came?

First Grade Essentials

142

How Many Left?

Directions: Solve each problem.

There are 10 white.
There are four blue.
How many more white than blue are there? __6__

$$\begin{array}{r} 10 \\ -\ 4 \\ \hline 6 \end{array}$$

Ten are on the table.
Two are broken.
How many are not broken? __8__

$$\begin{array}{r} 10 \\ -\ 2 \\ \hline 8 \end{array}$$

There are nine.
Six swim away.
How many are left? __3__

$$\begin{array}{r} 9 \\ -\ 6 \\ \hline 3 \end{array}$$

Joni wants nine.
She has five.
How many more does she need? __4__

$$\begin{array}{r} 9 \\ -\ 5 \\ \hline 4 \end{array}$$

There were 10.
Five melted.
How many did not melt? __5__

$$\begin{array}{r} 10 \\ -\ 5 \\ \hline 5 \end{array}$$

One Step Further
What color flowers are outside your home? Draw a picture of your favorite flower.

First Grade Essentials

143

How Many Animals Are Left?

Directions: The key word **left** tells you to subtract. Circle the key word **left**. Write a number sentence to solve each subtraction problem.

1. Bill had 10 kittens, but four of them ran away. How many kittens does he have (left)?

   10 − 4 = 6

2. There were 12 rabbits eating in the garden. Dogs chased three of them away. How many rabbits were (left)?

   12 − 3 = 9

3. There were 14 frogs on the bank of the pond. Then, nine of them hopped into the water. How many frogs were (left) on the bank?

   14 − 9 = 5

4. Bill saw 11 birds eating from the bird feeders in his backyard. A cat scared seven of them away. How many birds were (left) at the feeders?

   11 − 7 = 4

5. Bill counted 15 robins in his yard. Then, eight of the robins flew away. How many robins were (left) in the yard?

   15 − 8 = 7

One Step Further
Is there a bird feeder in your yard? How many birds are eating from the feeder?

First Grade Essentials

144

Fish Bowl

Directions: Color **20** fish. Circle to show how many fish are left over.

(5) 6 7

Coloring may vary.

One Step Further
Go to a pet store. How many fish tanks are there? How many fish are in each tank?

145

Frog Fun

Directions: Color **22** frogs. Circle to show how many frogs are left over.

3 (4) 5

Coloring may vary.

One Step Further
If there are **22** frogs and **7** lily pads, how many frogs do not have a lily pad to sit on?

First Grade Essentials

ANSWER KEY

MATH

146

Snail Garden

Directions: Color **25** snails 🐌. Circle to show how many snails are left over.

③ 4 5

Coloring may vary.

One Step Further
Use three words to describe a snail. Have you ever seen a snail in your yard?

First Grade Essentials

147

Working on Webs

Directions: Color **25** spiders 🕷. Circle to show how many spiders are left over.

1 ② 3

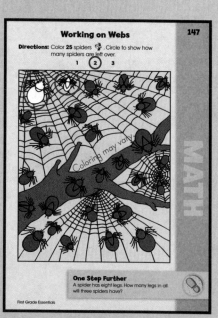

Coloring may vary.

One Step Further
A spider has eight legs. How many legs in all will three spiders have?

First Grade Essentials

148

Picture Problems

Directions: Solve the number problem under each picture. Write **+** or **–** to show if you should add or subtract.

How many ⛄ in all?   How many 🦇s are left?

$7 + 5 = \underline{12}$ $8 - 3 = \underline{5}$

How many ❀s are left?   How many 🎄s in all?

$9 - 4 = \underline{5}$ $14 + 1 = \underline{15}$

How many ✏s are left?   How many ●s in all?

$15 - 6 = \underline{9}$ $9 + 5 = \underline{14}$

One Step Further
Grab some pencils. Take away three of them. How many are left?

First Grade Essentials

149

Puppy Problems

Directions: Look at the pictures. Complete the number sentences.

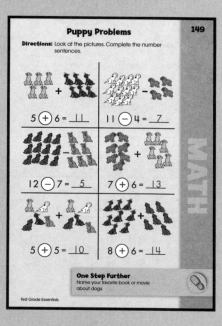

$5 \,⊕\, 6 = \underline{11}$ $11 \,⊖\, 4 = \underline{7}$

$12 \,⊖\, 7 = \underline{5}$ $7 \,⊕\, 6 = \underline{13}$

$5 \,⊕\, 5 = \underline{10}$ $8 \,⊕\, 6 = \underline{14}$

One Step Further
Name your favorite book or movie about dogs.

First Grade Essentials

150

Addition and Subtraction

Directions: Solve the problems.

$1 + 3 = \underline{4}$ $4 - 3 = \underline{1}$ $4 + 5 = \underline{9}$

$6 + 1 = \underline{7}$ $7 - 2 = \underline{5}$ $8 - 4 = \underline{4}$

$9 - 1 = \underline{8}$ $10 - 3 = \underline{7}$

$5 - 2 = \underline{3}$ $6 + 3 = \underline{9}$

$8 + 2 = \underline{10}$ $5 + 5 = \underline{10}$

One Step Further
What is your favorite zoo animal? What do you like about it?

First Grade Essentials

151

Add or Subtract?

Directions: The key words **in all** tell you to add. The key word **left** tells you to subtract. Circle the key words and write **+** or **–** in the circles. Then, solve the problems.

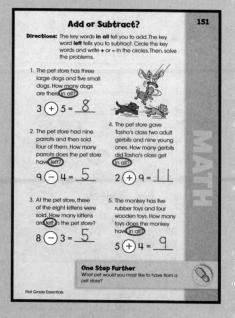

1. The pet store has three large dogs and five small dogs. How many dogs are there (in all)?

$3 \,⊕\, 5 = \underline{8}$

2. The pet store had nine parrots and then sold four of them. How many parrots does the pet store have (left)?

$9 \,⊖\, 4 = \underline{5}$

3. At the pet store, three of the eight kittens were sold. How many kittens are (left) in the pet store?

$8 \,⊖\, 3 = \underline{5}$

4. The pet store gave Tasha's class two adult gerbils and nine young ones. How many gerbils did Tasha's class get (in all)?

$2 \,⊕\, 9 = \underline{11}$

5. The monkey has five rubber toys and four wooden toys. How many toys does the monkey have (in all)?

$5 \,⊕\, 4 = \underline{9}$

One Step Further
What pet would you most like to have from a pet store?

First Grade Essentials

---

152 **Helen the Housefly**

Directions: Connect the dots from **0** to **100**. Color the picture.

One Step Further
Write a story about why flies buzz in people's ears.

First Grade Essentials

---

153 **Chris the Cricket**

Directions: Connect the dots from **15** to **100**. Color the picture.

One Step Further
Crickets chirp. With a friend, use different kinds of chirps to make up a secret code.

First Grade Essentials

---

154 **Scotty the Stag Beetle**

Directions: Connect the dots from **50** to **200**. Color the picture.

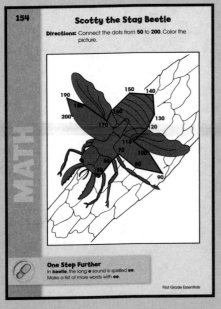

One Step Further
In **beetle**, the long **e** sound is spelled **ee**. Make a list of more words with **ee**.

First Grade Essentials

---

155 **Barry the Beetle**

Directions: Connect the dots from **10** to **200**. Color the picture.

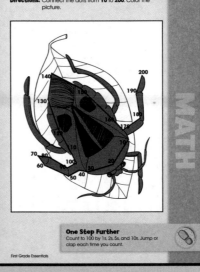

One Step Further
Count to 100 by 1s, 2s, 5s, and 10s. Jump or clap each time you count.

First Grade Essentials

---

156 **Sizable Patterns**

Directions: Look at each pattern. Connect the missing picture to each pattern. Not all pictures will be used.

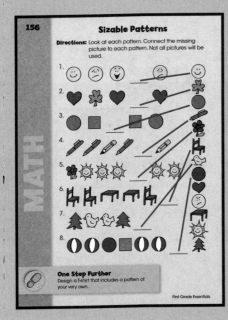

One Step Further
Design a T-shirt that includes a pattern of your very own.

First Grade Essentials

---

157 **Square, Square, Circle**

Directions: Look at the patterns. Draw in each missing shape.

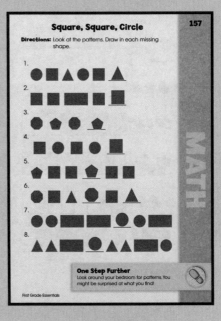

One Step Further
Look around your bedroom for patterns. You might be surprised at what you find!

First Grade Essentials

MATH

ANSWER KEY

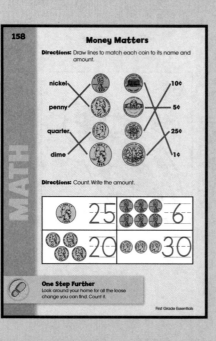

158 — Money Matters

Directions: Draw lines to match each coin to its name and amount.

nickel — penny — quarter — dime
10¢ — 5¢ — 25¢ — 1¢

Directions: Count. Write the amount.

25   6
20   30

One Step Further
Look around your home for all the loose change you can find. Count it.

First Grade Essentials

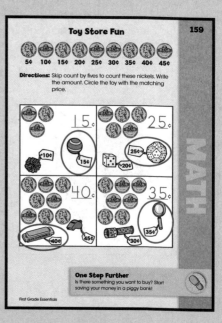

159 — Toy Store Fun

5¢ 10¢ 15¢ 20¢ 25¢ 30¢ 35¢ 40¢ 45¢

Directions: Skip count by fives to count these nickels. Write the amount. Circle the toy with the matching price.

15¢   25¢
40¢   35¢

One Step Further
Is there something you want to buy? Start saving your money in a piggy bank!

First Grade Essentials

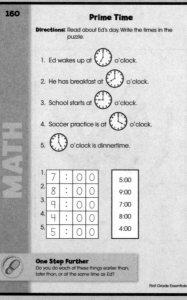

160 — Prime Time

Directions: Read about Ed's day. Write the times in the puzzle.

1. Ed wakes up at ⬚ o'clock.
2. He has breakfast at ⬚ o'clock.
3. School starts at ⬚ o'clock.
4. Soccer practice is at ⬚ o'clock.
5. ⬚ o'clock is dinnertime.

1. 7 : 0 0
2. 8 : 0 0
3. 9 : 0 0
4. 4 : 0 0
5. 5 : 0 0

5:00
9:00
7:00
8:00
4:00

One Step Further
Do you do each of these things earlier than, later than, or at the same time as Ed?

First Grade Essentials

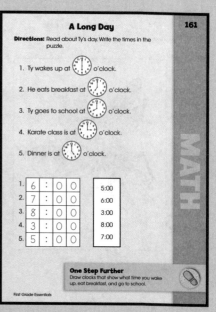

161 — A Long Day

Directions: Read about Ty's day. Write the times in the puzzle.

1. Ty wakes up at ⬚ o'clock.
2. He eats breakfast at ⬚ o'clock.
3. Ty goes to school at ⬚ o'clock.
4. Karate class is at ⬚ o'clock.
5. Dinner is at ⬚ o'clock.

1. 6 : 0 0
2. 7 : 0 0
3. 8 : 0 0
4. 3 : 0 0
5. 5 : 0 0

5:00
6:00
3:00
8:00
7:00

One Step Further
Draw clocks that show what time you wake up, eat breakfast, and go to school.

First Grade Essentials

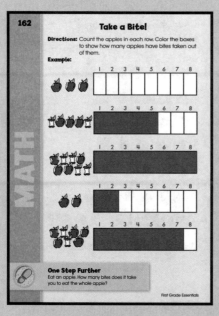

162 — Take a Bite!

Directions: Count the apples in each row. Color the boxes to show how many apples have bites taken out of them.

Example:

1 2 3 4 5 6 7 8

One Step Further
Eat an apple. How many bites does it take you to eat the whole apple?

First Grade Essentials

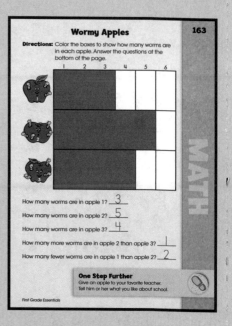

163 — Wormy Apples

Directions: Color the boxes to show how many worms are in each apple. Answer the questions at the bottom of the page.

1 2 3 4 5 6

How many worms are in apple 1? 3
How many worms are in apple 2? 5
How many worms are in apple 3? 4
How many more worms are in apple 2 than apple 3? 1
How many fewer worms are in apple 1 than apple 2? 2

One Step Further
Give an apple to your favorite teacher. Tell him or her what you like about school.

First Grade Essentials

164 — Graphing

Directions: Complete the graph below. Use the number of each animal you counted to fill in the rows with the missing pictures of turtles and dogs. The giraffes and sheep have been filled in for you.

Which animal cracker is there the most of? **giraffe**

Which animal cracker is there the fewest of? **sheep, turtle, dog**

Three kinds of crackers have the same number. How many are there? **2**

One Step Further
Open a box of animal crackers. Make a graph of the animals in the box.

First Grade Essentials

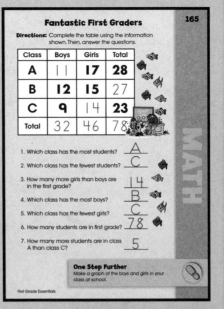

165 — Fantastic First Graders

Directions: Complete the table using the information shown. Then, answer the questions.

Class	Boys	Girls	Total
A	11	17	28
B	12	15	27
C	9	14	23
Total	32	46	78

1. Which class has the most students? **A**
2. Which class has the fewest students? **C**
3. How many more girls than boys are in the first grade? **14**
4. Which class has the most boys? **B**
5. Which class has the fewest girls? **C**
6. How many students are in first grade? **78**
7. How many more students are in class A than class C? **5**

One Step Further
Make a graph of the boys and girls in your class at school.

First Grade Essentials

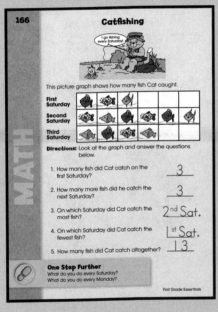

166 — Catfishing

I go fishing every Saturday!

This picture graph shows how many fish Cat caught.

First Saturday					
Second Saturday					
Third Saturday					

Directions: Look at the graph and answer the questions below.

1. How many fish did Cat catch on the first Saturday? **3**
2. How many more fish did he catch the next Saturday? **3**
3. On which Saturday did Cat catch the most fish? **2nd Sat.**
4. On which Saturday did Cat catch the fewest fish? **1st Sat.**
5. How many fish did Cat catch altogether? **13**

One Step Further
What do you do every Saturday? What do you do every Monday?

First Grade Essentials

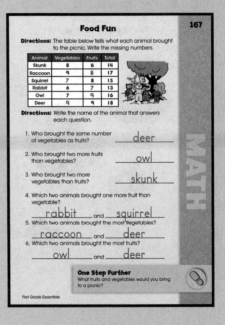

167 — Food Fun

Directions: The table below tells what each animal brought to the picnic. Write the missing numbers.

Animal	Vegetables	Fruits	Total
Skunk	8	6	14
Raccoon	9	8	17
Squirrel	7	8	15
Rabbit	6	7	13
Owl	7	9	16
Deer	9	9	18

Directions: Write the name of the animal that answers each question.

1. Who brought the same number of vegetables as fruits? **deer**
2. Who brought two more fruits than vegetables? **owl**
3. Who brought two more vegetables than fruits? **skunk**
4. Which two animals brought one more fruit than vegetable? **rabbit** and **squirrel**
5. Which two animals brought the most vegetables? **raccoon** and **deer**
6. Which two animals brought the most fruits? **owl** and **deer**

One Step Further
What fruits and vegetables would you bring to a picnic?

First Grade Essentials

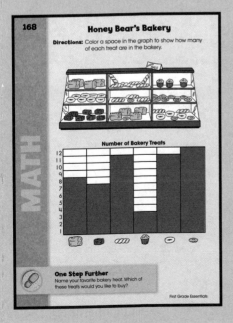

168 — Honey Bear's Bakery

Directions: Color a space in the graph to show how many of each treat are in the bakery.

Number of Bakery Treats

One Step Further
Name your favorite bakery treat. Which of these treats would you like to buy?

First Grade Essentials

169 — Amy's Things

Directions: Count the toys on Amy's shelf. Complete the table. Then, answer the questions.

Toy	How Many?
Dolls	4
Teddy Bears	4
Blocks	5
Pigs	1
Books	7
Cars	3

1. How many books and pigs are there altogether? **8**
2. How many more teddy bears are there than cars? **1**
3. Are there more dolls or animals? **animals**
4. Amy has four more **books/blocks** than **cars/pigs**
5. Are there enough cars for each doll? **no**

One Step Further
How many kinds of toys are on your toy shelf? What toy do you have the most of?

First Grade Essentials

ANSWER KEY

170 — Inch

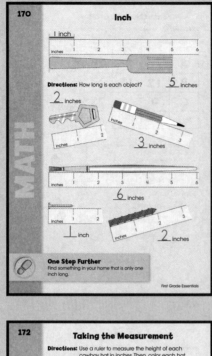

1 inch

Directions: How long is each object?

5 inches

2 inches

3 inches

1 inch

6 inches

1 inch

2 inches

One Step Further
Find something in your home that is only one inch long.

First Grade Essentials

171 — Centimeter

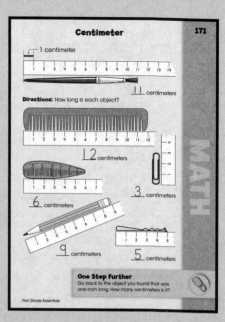

1 centimeter

11 centimeters

Directions: How long is each object?

12 centimeters

3 centimeters

6 centimeters

9 centimeters

5 centimeters

One Step Further
Go back to the object you found that was one inch long. How many centimeters is it?

First Grade Essentials

172 — Taking the Measurement

Directions: Use a ruler to measure the height of each cowboy hat in inches. Then, color each hat according to the chart.

Height	Color
0-1	brown
1½-3	green

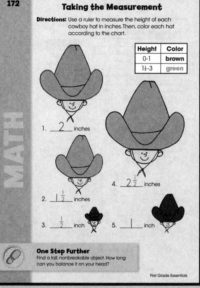

1. 2 inches
2. 1½ inches
3. ½ inch
4. 2½ inches
5. 1 inch

One Step Further
Find a tall, nonbreakable object. How long can you balance it on your head?

First Grade Essentials

173 — Flowers That "Measure" Up

Directions: Use a centimeter ruler to measure how tall each flower is. Measure each flower from the bottom of the stem to the top of the flower. Write the answer on the blank by the flower.

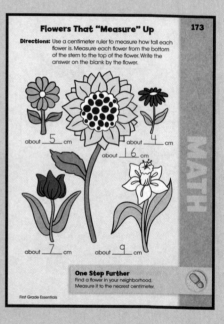

about 5 cm

about 4 cm

about 6 cm

about 7 cm

about 9 cm

One Step Further
Find a flower in your neighborhood. Measure it to the nearest centimeter.

First Grade Essentials

174 — How Far Is It?

Directions: Use a ruler to measure each distance on the map in inches. Then, use the letters on the circles and your answers to solve the message at the bottom of the page.

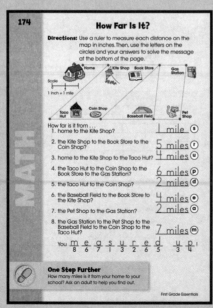

Scale
1 inch = 1 mile

How far is it from . . .
1. home to the Kite Shop? — 1 mile (s)
2. the Kite Shop to the Book Store to the Coin Shop? — 5 miles (r)
3. home to the Kite Shop to the Taco Hut? — 4 miles (u)
4. the Taco Hut to the Coin Shop to the Book Store to the Gas Station? — 6 miles (p)
5. the Taco Hut to the Coin Shop? — 2 miles (d)
6. the Baseball Field to the Book Store to the Kite Shop? — 4 miles (e)
7. the Pet Shop to the Gas Station? — 2 miles (a)
8. the Gas Station to the Pet Shop to the Baseball Field to the Coin Shop to the Taco Hut? — 7 miles (m)

You m e a s u r e d   u p !
8 6 7 1 3 2 6 5   3 4

One Step Further
How many miles is it from your home to your school? Ask an adult to help you find out.

First Grade Essentials

175 — Whole and Half

A **fraction** is a number that names part of a whole, such as ½ or ⅓.

Directions: Color half of each object.

Example:

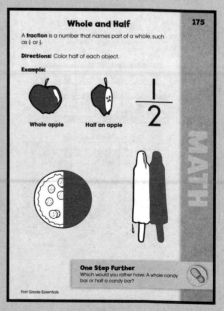

Whole apple

Half an apple

$\frac{1}{2}$

One Step Further
Which would you rather have: A whole candy bar or half a candy bar?

First Grade Essentials

First Grade Essentials

ANSWER KEY

176 — Thirds

Directions: Circle the objects that have three equal parts.

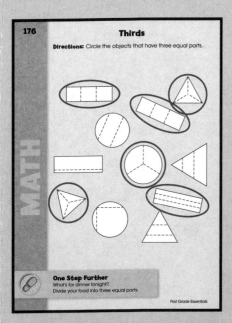

One Step Further
What's for dinner tonight?
Divide your food into three equal parts.

First Grade Essentials

177 — Fourths

Directions: Circle the objects that have four equal parts.

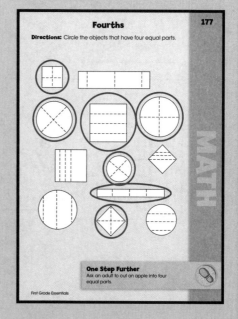

One Step Further
Ask an adult to cut an apple into four equal parts.

First Grade Essentials

179 — Fractions

Directions: Answer the questions and fill in the blanks below. The first one is done for you.

How many monsters touch their toes?
$\underline{1}$ out of 10 monsters, or $\dfrac{1}{10}$ of the monsters.

How many monsters hang upside down?
$\underline{3}$ out of 10 monsters, or $\dfrac{3}{10}$ of the monsters.

How many of the monsters ride the bikes?
$\underline{2}$ out of 10 monsters, or $\dfrac{2}{10}$ of the monsters.

How many of the monsters run on the treadmill?
$\underline{1}$ out of 10 monsters, or $\dfrac{1}{10}$ of the monsters.

How many monsters lift weights?
$\underline{2}$ out of 10 monsters, or $\dfrac{2}{10}$ of the monsters.

How many monsters do leg lifts?
$\underline{1}$ out of 10 monsters, or $\dfrac{1}{10}$ of the monsters.

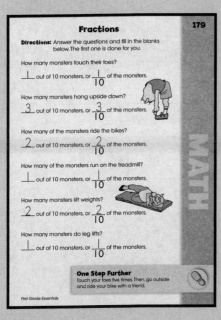

One Step Further
Touch your toes five times. Then, go outside and ride your bike with a friend.

First Grade Essentials

180 — Review

Directions: Count the equal parts. Then, write the fraction.

Example:

Shaded part = $\underline{1}$ Equal parts = $\underline{3}$ Write $\dfrac{1}{3}$

Shaded part = $\underline{1}$ Equal parts = $\underline{2}$ Write $\dfrac{1}{2}$

Shaded part = $\underline{1}$ Equal parts = $\underline{3}$ Write $\dfrac{1}{3}$

Shaded part = $\underline{1}$ Equal parts = $\underline{4}$ Write $\dfrac{1}{4}$

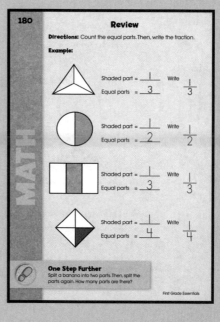

One Step Further
Split a banana into two parts. Then, split the parts again. How many parts are there?

First Grade Essentials

182 — Healthy Foods

Directions: Read the clues and use the words in the word box to complete the puzzle.

Word box: fruit, vegetable, bread, milk, meat

Across
2. A bagel is a food from the ___ and cereal group.
3. A slice of cheese belongs to the ___ group.
4. An orange is a food from the ___ group.

Down
1. Broccoli is a food from the ___ group.
3. Chicken and eggs belong to the ___ group.

One Step Further
Say a color name. Can a friend think of healthy foods which have that color?

First Grade Essentials

183 — Things to Eat

Directions: Use the code to help you spell the food words.

1. $\underset{8}{p}\,\underset{4}{e}\,\underset{4}{a}\,\underset{9}{r}$ — pear
2. $\underset{10}{s}\,\underset{11}{t}\,\underset{4}{e}\,\underset{1}{a}\,\underset{5}{k}$ — steak
3. $\underset{3}{c}\,\underset{7}{o}\,\underset{9}{r}\,\underset{6}{n}$ — corn
4. $\underset{2}{b}\,\underset{1}{a}\,\underset{6}{n}\,\underset{1}{a}\,\underset{6}{n}\,\underset{1}{a}$ — banana
5. $\underset{2}{b}\,\underset{1}{a}\,\underset{3}{c}\,\underset{7}{o}\,\underset{6}{n}$ — bacon
6. $\underset{11}{t}\,\underset{7}{o}\,\underset{1}{a}\,\underset{10}{s}\,\underset{11}{t}$ — toast
7. $\underset{3}{c}\,\underset{1}{a}\,\underset{5}{k}\,\underset{4}{e}$ — cake

Code: a 1, b 2, c 3, e 4, k 5, n 6, o 7, p 8, r 9, s 10, t 11

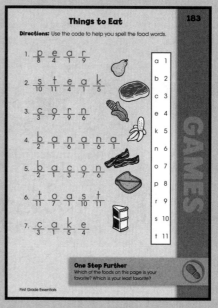

One Step Further
Which of the foods on this page is your favorite? Which is your least favorite?

First Grade Essentials

First Grade Essentials

ANSWER KEY

GAMES GAMES GAMES GAMES GAMES GAMES

---

184 — **On the Shore**

Directions: Circle the words in the puzzle. The words go across and down.

ship	sand	sun	shine
shells	shore	sail	swim

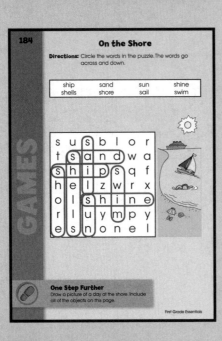

One Step Further
Draw a picture of a day at the shore. Include all of the objects on this page.

First Grade Essentials

---

185 — **Fishy Friends**

Directions: Help the striped fish swim through the coral and find its friend.

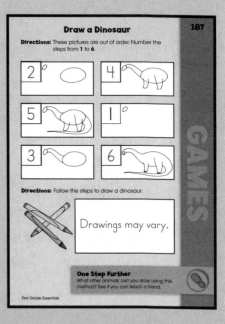

One Step Further
Who is your best friend? Draw a picture of the two of you on the day you met.

First Grade Essentials

---

186 — **Dinosaurs**

Directions: Read the clues and use the words in the word box to complete the puzzle.

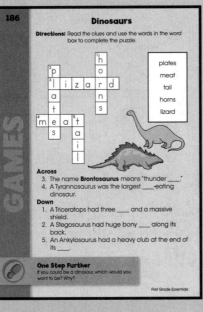

Word box: plates, meat, tail, horns, lizard

Across
3. The name **Brontosaurus** means "thunder ____."
4. A Tyrannosaurus was the largest ____-eating dinosaur.

Down
1. A Triceratops had three ____ and a massive shield.
2. A Stegosaurus had huge bony ____ along its back.
5. An Ankylosaurus had a heavy club at the end of its ____.

One Step Further
If you could be a dinosaur, which would you want to be? Why?

First Grade Essentials

---

187 — **Draw a Dinosaur**

Directions: These pictures are out of order. Number the steps from **1** to **6**.

2 · 4 · 5 · 1 · 3 · 6

Directions: Follow the steps to draw a dinosaur.

Drawings may vary.

One Step Further
What other animals can you draw using this method? See if you can teach a friend.

First Grade Essentials

---

188 — **Mail Delivery**

Directions: Lead the pig to the mailbox.

One Step Further
What is the best thing you've ever gotten in the mail?

First Grade Essentials

---

189 — **Mail Call**

Directions: Unscramble the words that have to do with mail.

1. retties — letters
2. cpageksa — packages
3. tpamss — stamps
4. ilam rrcaire — mail carrier
5. tsop oceiff — post office
6. axombil — mailbox
7. leeydivr — delivery
8. dracs — cards

delivery	mail carrier	
letters	stamps	packages
mailbox	cards	post office

One Step Further
Write a friendly letter to a friend or family member. Ask an adult to help you mail it.

First Grade Essentials

First Grade Essentials

190 — Park the Car

Directions: Drive the car to the garage.

One Step Further
Create a map of the street you live on. Include landmarks like trees and stop signs.

First Grade Essentials

---

191 — A Neighborhood

Directions: Read the clues and use the words in the word box to complete the puzzle.

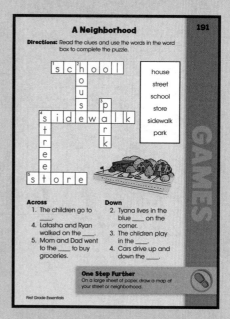

Word box: house, street, school, store, sidewalk, park

Crossword answers:
- 1. school
- 2. house
- 3. park
- 4. sidewalk / street
- 5. store

Across
1. The children go to ____.
4. Latasha and Ryan walked on the ____.
5. Mom and Dad went to the ____ to buy groceries.

Down
2. Tyana lives in the blue ____ on the corner.
3. The children play in the ____.
4. Cars drive up and down the ____.

One Step Further
On a large sheet of paper, draw a map of your street or neighborhood.

First Grade Essentials

---

192 — Toy Time

Directions: Circle the words in the puzzle. The words go across and down.

```
b t r a i n b a t x
i g t c d g a m e p
k a o e b a l l n c
e t p f h k r m o s
d o l l p t s p q z
j k o b l o c k l p
```

train, bat, doll, bike, block, ball, top, game

One Step Further
Gather up some of your old toys and donate them to someone in need.

First Grade Essentials

---

193 — Time to Clean Up

Directions: Take the toys to the toy box.

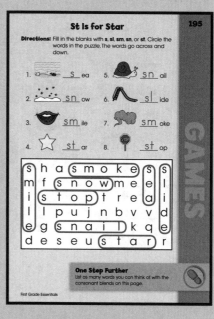

One Step Further
Go through some old toys or books. You might discover a fond memory!

First Grade Essentials

---

194 — Shining Bright

Directions: To find the mystery letter, color the spaces with the following letters red.

Q F V P G O M N U S

```
Q G M N
S A J W
U F P H
O L T Z
V Y R B
```

Directions: Circle the mystery letter.

E **F** P

One Step Further
Name five objects that you could describe as shiny.

First Grade Essentials

---

195 — St Is for Star

Directions: Fill in the blanks with **s, sl, sm, sn,** or **st.** Circle the words in the puzzle. The words go across and down.

1. _s_ ea
2. _sn_ ow
3. _sm_ ile
4. _st_ ar
5. _sn_ ail
6. _sl_ ide
7. _sm_ oke
8. _st_ op

```
s h a s m o k e s s
m f s n o w m e e l
i s t o p t r e a i
l l p u j n b v v d
e g s n a i l k q e
d e s e u s t a r r
```

One Step Further
List as many words you can think of with the consonant blends on this page.

First Grade Essentials

ANSWER KEY

196

At the Beach

Directions: Read the clues and use the words in the word box to complete the puzzle.

Crossword answers:
- ¹d
- ²ships / s / ³hat
- h / g / o
- e / ⁴r
- ⁵ball / r
- ⁶large

Word box:
ships, shore, shell, dig, ball, large, hat

Across
2. I saw three ___ sail by.
4. I wore a ___ to protect myself from the sun.
5. I played catch with my beach ___.
6. I even saw a dolphin that was very ___.

Down
1. I used a shovel to ___ in the sand.
2. I found a ___ at the beach.
3. I saw a ship float up onto the ___.

One Step Further
Tell a story about a day at the beach. Make up characters for your story.

First Grade Essentials

197

Underwater

Directions: Circle the words in the puzzle. The words go across and down.

Word search grid:
```
g l w o t b d c f s r a
s e a l s f o t i e w o
h a t w h a l e s a x p
e b p a r t p j h w z l
l y l t i d h e z e f a
l b t e m e i m x e b n
s r g r p q n e o d l t
a o n l e x s h a r k s
```

water, seals, sharks, fish, shrimp, plants, shells, whales, dolphins, seaweed

One Step Further
What is your favorite underwater creature? Have you ever seen one in real life?

First Grade Essentials

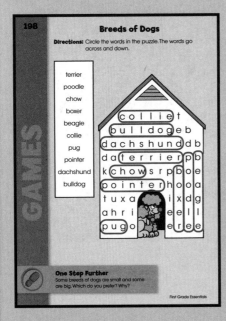

198

Breeds of Dogs

Directions: Circle the words in the puzzle. The words go across and down.

terrier, poodle, chow, boxer, beagle, collie, pug, pointer, dachshund, bulldog

Word search grid:
```
c o l l i e t
b u l l d o g e b
d a c h s h u n d d b
d a t e r r i e r p b
k c h o w s r p b o e
p o i n t e r h o o a
t u x a i x d g
a h r i e e l l
p u g o e r e e
```

One Step Further
Some breeds of dogs are small and some are big. Which do you prefer? Why?

First Grade Essentials

199

Lost Collar

Directions: Help the puppy find its collar.

One Step Further
Design a fancy doghouse. What could you put inside?

First Grade Essentials

200

Crack the Code

Directions: Use the code to write the missing letters for each word.

1. c ___ r ___ ayon
2. m ___ ou ___ s ___ e
3. m ___ oon
4. ___ s ___ ta ___ r
5. ___ c ___ lou ___ d
6. ___ c ___ a ___ r ___ r ___ ot
7. bi ___ r ___ d
8. ___ m ___ on ___ k ___ ey

Code:
c ●
r ☆
s ▲
m ⬠
d ▪
k ◆

One Step Further
Create symbols for all letters of the alphabet. Write a message using your symbols.

First Grade Essentials

201

Fix These Words

Directions: Unscramble the letters. Use the pictures to help you. Write the words on the lines.

g p i	pig	r a t s	star
u n s	sun	d e b	bed
t h a	hat	n f a	fan
t e n s	nest	u b s	bus

One Step Further
Look outside and write five things you see. Scramble their names and let a friend solve.

First Grade Essentials

First Grade Essentials

GAMES

202 — Picture Clues

Directions: Letters, numbers, and pictures take the place of words in each sentence below. Write each sentence correctly.

R	are	🥫	can	U	you
8	ate	👁	I	m👁	my

1. 👁 8 an apple.

   I ate an apple.

2. R U happy?

   Are you happy?

3. 🥫 U see me?

   Can you see me?

4. 👁 🥫 see U

   I can see you.

One Step Further
Write a message to a friend using the code. Create other symbols if you want to.

First Grade Essentials

203 — Secret Word

Directions: Use the clues to help you fill in the puzzles.

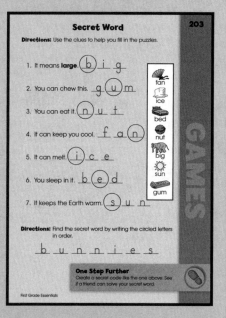

1. It means **large**. b i g
2. You can chew this. g u m
3. You can eat it. n u t
4. It can keep you cool. f a n
5. It can melt. i c e
6. You sleep in it. b e d
7. It keeps the Earth warm. s u n

Picture word box: fan, ice, bed, nut, big, sun, gum

Directions: Find the secret word by writing the circled letters in order.

b u n n i e s

One Step Further
Create a secret code like the one above. See if a friend can solve your secret word.

First Grade Essentials

204 — At the Pet Shop

Directions: Read the clues and use the words in the word box to complete the puzzle.

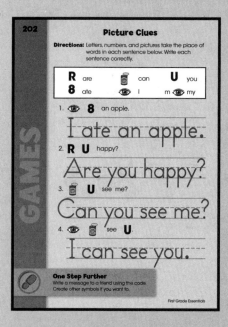

Crossword answers: bird, gerbil, fish, dog, cat, turtle, rabbit

Word box: dog, fish, cat, rabbit, turtle, gerbil, bird

Across
1. I have feathers. I can fly and sing.
4. I am small and furry with a long skinny tail. I like running around on a wheel.
7. I have a hard shell. I walk very slowly.

Down
2. I have fur. I can bark and do tricks.
3. I am very quiet. I swim in a bowl.
5. I have long floppy ears and a fluffy round tail. I like eating carrots.
6. I am furry. When you pet me I purr.

One Step Further
Write another riddle about a pet. See if a friend can guess the correct answer.

First Grade Essentials

205 — Pet Time

Directions: Look in the bone for the things you might need for a new pet. Write the words in the puzzle.

Crossword answers: treats, bones, collar, food, tank, blanket, bed, leash

Bone word box: leash, food, collar, treats, bones, bed, blanket

One Step Further
Taking care of a pet is hard work. What would a new puppy need each day?

First Grade Essentials

206 — All Dry

Directions: The clothes are dry. Help put them in the basket.

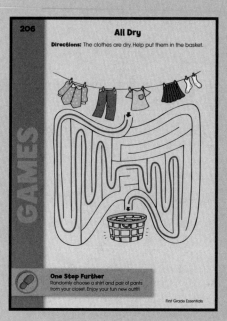

One Step Further
Randomly choose a shirt and pair of pants from your closet. Enjoy your fun new outfit!

First Grade Essentials

207 — Around the House

Directions: Read the clues and use the words in the word box to complete the puzzle.

Word box: locks, sink, bedroom, windows, porch, doors, kitchen, living room

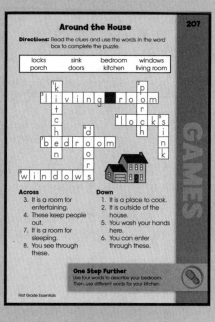

Crossword answers: living room, locks, bedroom, windows, kitchen, porch, doors, sink

Across
3. It is a room for entertaining.
4. These keep people out.
7. It is a room for sleeping.
8. You see through these.

Down
1. It is a place to cook.
2. It is outside of the house.
5. You wash your hands here.
6. You can enter through these.

One Step Further
Use four words to describe your bedroom. Then, use different words for your kitchen.

First Grade Essentials

208 — Safety

Directions: Read the clues and use the words in the word box to complete the puzzle.

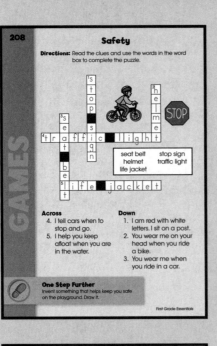

Word box:
seat belt   stop sign
helmet   traffic light
life jacket

Across
4. I tell cars when to stop and go.
5. I help you keep afloat when you are in the water.

Down
1. I am red with white letters. I sit on a post.
2. You wear me on your head when you ride a bike.
3. You wear me when you ride in a car.

One Step Further
Invent something that helps keep you safe on the playground. Draw it.

First Grade Essentials

209 — Being a Friend

Directions: Read the clues and use the words in the word box to complete the puzzle.

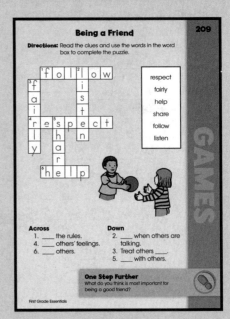

Word box:
respect
fairly
help
share
follow
listen

Across
1. _____ the rules.
4. _____ others' feelings.
6. _____ others.

Down
2. _____ when others are talking.
3. Treat others _____.
5. _____ with others.

One Step Further
What do you think is most important for being a good friend?

First Grade Essentials

210 — A Cold Walk

Directions: Help the penguin find its way to the igloo.

One Step Further
Igloo begins and ends with a vowel. Name other words that follow this pattern.

First Grade Essentials

211 — Scott's Sled

Directions: Show Scott the trail to his sled.

One Step Further
What is your favorite winter activity? Do you prefer being indoors or outdoors?

First Grade Essentials

First Grade Essentials

212   Field Goal

Directions: Kick the football through the goalposts.

One Step Further
Choreograph your own touchdown dance. Perform it until you have it memorized.

First Grade Essentials

---

213   Figure Them Out!

Directions: Unscramble each word. Be sure that it matches the meaning.

teacher	ice cream	apple
mouse	jogger	tennis

1. Someone who runs is called a
   rjggeo j o g g e r.
2. A game that uses a racket and a small ball is
   stinne t e n n i s.
3. Something cold to eat on a hot day is
   cie ramec i c e   c r e a m.
4. Someone who teaches children is a
   erhteac t e a c h e r.
5. A tasty fruit that grows on a tree is called an
   leppa a p p l e.
6. A furry little animal that squeaks is a
   somue m o u s e.

One Step Further
Scramble five more words for a friend. Give him or her clues to help find the answer.

First Grade Essentials

---

214   In a City

Directions: Read the clues and use the words in the word box to complete the puzzle.

m a l l   h z o o
u   s
s k y s c r a p e r
e   u   i
u   b u s   t
m   w   t a x i
  a
  y

Word box: subway, skyscraper, hospital, museum, taxi, mall, bus, zoo

Across
2. This is a place with many stores in one building.
3. This is a place where many animals live.
4. This is a very tall building.
6. Many people ride in this on city streets.
7. People whistle, yell, or wave to get a ride in this thing.

Down
1. This is a place where people go when they are sick.
2. People visit this place to see very old things.
5. This train goes underground and people ride it.

One Step Further
What large city is near your home? Find it on a map.

First Grade Essentials

---

215   Around the World

Directions: Read the clues and use the words in the word box to complete the puzzle.

Word box: glacier, ocean, mountain, continent, desert

d
m   e
c o n t i n e n t
u   s
o c e a n   r
t   t
g l a c i e r
i
n

Across
3. A very large area of land
4. A very large body of water
5. A river of ice that seems to stand still

Down
1. A hot, dry area
2. A very high hill

One Step Further
There are seven continents and four oceans. How many can you name?

First Grade Essentials

GAMES

216 — Things That Are Alike

Directions: Read the clues and find the other things from the word box that go with each group to complete the puzzle.

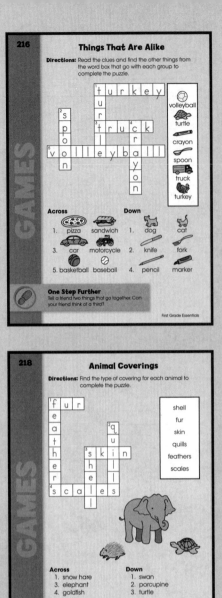

Word box: volleyball, turtle, crayon, spoon, truck, turkey

Crossword answers:
- 1 (across): turkey
- 2 (down): spoon
- 3 (across): truck
- 5 (across): volleyball
- (down): turtle, crayon, turkey

Across
1. pizza sandwich
3. car motorcycle
5. basketball baseball

Down
1. dog cat
2. knife fork
4. pencil marker

One Step Further
Tell a friend two things that go together. Can your friend think of a third?

First Grade Essentials

217 — Musical Instruments

Directions: Use the code to find out which instruments the children play.

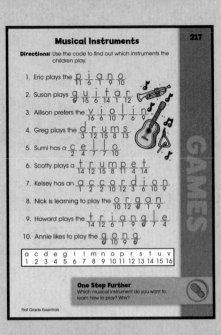

1. Eric plays the p i a n o
   11 6 1 9 10
2. Susan plays g u i t a r
   5 15 6 14 1 12
3. Allison prefers the v i o l i n
   16 6 10 7 6 9
4. Greg plays the d r u m s
   3 12 15 8 13
5. Sumi has a c e l l o
   2 4 7 7 10
6. Scotty plays a t r u m p e t
   14 12 15 8 11 4 14
7. Kelsey has an a c c o r d i o n
   1 2 2 10 12 3 6 10 9
8. Nick is learning to play the o r g a n
   10 12 5 1 9
9. Howard plays the t r i a n g l e
   14 12 6 1 9 5 7 4
10. Annie likes to play the g o n g
    5 10 9 5

a	c	d	e	g	i	l	m	n	o	p	r	s	t	u	v
1	2	3	4	5	6	7	8	9	10	11	12	13	14	15	16

One Step Further
Which musical instrument do you want to learn how to play? Why?

First Grade Essentials

218 — Animal Coverings

Directions: Find the type of covering for each animal to complete the puzzle.

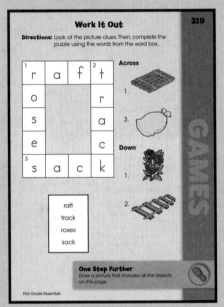

Crossword answers:
- 1: fur
- (down): feathers
- 2 (down): quills
- 3: skin, shell
- 4: scales

Word box: shell, fur, skin, quills, feathers, scales

Across
1. snow hare
3. elephant
4. goldfish

Down
1. swan
2. porcupine
3. turtle

One Step Further
Which covering would you like to have for a day: quills, feathers, or scales? Why?

First Grade Essentials

219 — Work It Out

Directions: Look at the picture clues. Then, complete the puzzle using the words from the word box.

Crossword answers:
- 1 (across): raft
- 1 (down): roses
- 2 (down): track
- 3 (across): sack

Across
1.
3.

Down
1.
2.

Word box: raft, track, roses, sack

One Step Further
Draw a picture that includes all the objects on this page.

First Grade Essentials